DOLLARS AND SENSE FOR COLLEGE STUDENTS

OR HOW NOT TO RUN OUT
OF MONEY BY MID-TERMS

DOLLARS AND SENSE FOR COLLEGE STUDENTS

or How <u>Not</u> to Run Out of Money by Mid-terms

by Ellen Braitman

Random House, Inc.
New York
www.randomhouse.com

Princeton Review Publishing, L.L.C.
2315 Broadway, 3rd Floor
New York, NY 10024

ISBN 0-375-75206-4

Editor: Celeste Sollod
Production Editor: James Petrozzello
Designer: John Bergdahl

Manufactured in the United States of America.

9   8   7   6   5

First Edition

Dedication

For David

Acknowledgments

I've long maintained that being a journalist is a great job because those of us in the field get paid to ask questions and master new topics. So I am indebted to every editor who has given me the opportunity to report stories for a living and all the individuals who have given me their time so that I could interview them.

As a personal finance writer, I've gained great insight into how to manage my own financial life. The first and most important lessons I learned, however, did not come from reporting. They came from my parents, who supported me during the years I was a student and taught me to pay my bills on time.

Celeste Sollod came to me with the idea for this book and has been a skillful editor. My friend Colleen Kapklein gave me wise counsel and encouragement during the entire process. My brother Gary offered invaluable comments on the manuscript. Lesly Atlas offered eleventh-hour help. James Petrozello, Matthew Reilly, and Iam Williams sheparded the book through production. Peter DeGiglio, Kate Larkin, Mary Beth Roche, Kathy Schneider, and Evan Schnittman championed my work. My husband David gives me the constant support and love that make each day worthwhile.

To each of them, I am grateful.

Contents

Introduction

Money Matters

Money. You've heard a lot about it. It doesn't grow on trees. It burns a hole in your pocket. It makes the world go round. Sometimes you've got it, sometimes you don't. If you've just headed off to college, your parents have probably taken care of most of your financial needs until now. They supply food, shelter, and some or all of your clothing. You might even be lucky enough to get them to pay for movies, concerts, CDs, and other entertainment. All that is probably about to change. Whether or not your parents are going to continue to finance your life, you're going to have to figure out how best to use your money; how to make sure you have enough cash to pay for food, clothing, tuition, shelter, and books, with a little left over for fun. That's where this book comes in. The Princeton Review has a lot of experience working with students heading off to college and graduate school, preparing them for everything from tests to life in the dorms. This book will show you how to deal with your personal finances. Hey, wait a second, you may be saying, I'm going to college, not Wall Street. Well, money still affects you. From buying pizza to notebooks to paying your next rent check or tuition bill, the amount of money in your wallet and bank account directly affects the purchase.

There are people who have three credit cards with thousands of dollars of debt on each and there are people who have no money left before the end of the semester because they blew all their funds during the first few weeks of the term. Wouldn't you rather be one of those confident, supremely unworried people who knows he has enough to pay rent for the next month, but can still buy that great sweater. You don't have to be another Bill Gates to make this happen. You just have to manage what you have. We'll show you how to plan your finances so that money doesn't become a big worry in your life. Personal finance is about managing your money—figuring out where your cash comes from and deciding how to spend it. That's right, not never spending it, just deciding what's important to you and spending it on that, rather than looking in your empty checking account and asking yourself, "Where did it all go?"

Many people find dealing with money daunting. But if you take the time now to master a handful of basic personal finance tips, you'll be set for life. Learn to use credit cards at age eighteen and you shouldn't run into debt woes when you're thirty-five. Figure out how to avoid unnecessary bank fees and ferret out the cheapest plane tickets when you're in college and you'll be on your way to making a lifetime of wise decisions.

Look around you. There are a lot of businesses that want your money. Open the pages of any campus paper and you're likely to see advertisements for gyms, tanning salons, restaurants, long-distance phone companies, and travel agents. Let's not forget credit cards. "Always Carry Protection," screams an advertisement from Citibank Visa, and MasterCard. And the word from Detroit? "Reward Yourself," proclaims an advertisement from GMAC, trying to entice you to buy a new car. A 1996 article in *USA Today* said advertisers would spend $57 million in that year alone pitching products to students on college campuses. The same article said students would spend a whopping $96 billion in 1996. The marketing onslaught for your consumer dollars starts when you're in college, so now is the best time to get a handle on how best to maneuver through the consumer world.

We'll show you how to best use your money through budgeting and making smart choices. We'll talk about credit cards, banks, food shopping, paying the rent, finding health insurance, and taxes. And of course, we'll talk about where you're going to get your money. The world of personal finance, however, isn't static. While everything in this book is current at the time of writing, it's important to remember that some details described here will change. Credit card companies often add new fees that cost consumers money. Banks change their minimum balance requirements and increase the cost of withdrawing money from the cash machine. Tax laws change.

The basics covered here, however, will give you a solid footing in handling your own financial life, from staving off debt to staving off starvation. Take a deep breath and remember—you're in control.

—Ellen Braitman

Chapter $1

If Money Doesn't Grow on Trees, Where Will I Get It?

That's a great question. As a student where will you get all the money you need to live? How can you learn to manage your money if you don't even have any to manage yet? Later chapters of this book will address how to handle all aspects of your personal finances once you have money. But first, we need to get a handle on what funds you actually have by the time you are enrolled in school (and during the entire time you spend there). For most students, college money comes from a combination of sources, including some or all of the following:

- Parents
- Gifts from grandparents and other people who wish to support your studies
- Personal savings
- Student loans
- Work-study jobs
- Part-time work and summer jobs
- Grants and scholarships

In this chapter, we'll talk about each of these sources of money—from figuring out how much may be available to giving suggestions about where to turn if you've exhausted family money and loans. This is not intended to be a thorough guide to financing the cost of your college education. The Princeton Review publishes *Paying for College Without Going Broke*, a great resource for anyone facing the challenge of paying for school. There are a number of other good books available, too. Plus, the Internet offers many sites that provide copious information on financing college. (Some of these are listed in the appendix at the end of the book.) Let's just briefly discuss where your money is coming from, especially the money that you'll need in addition to tuition.

Where to start: FAFSA

During the 1997-98 academic year, $55 billion in federal, state and private aid was available to help students get their college degrees in hand. So how do you make sure you get your fair share?

Unless you are sure that your family can afford it and plans to pay for your schooling outright, the first step in figuring out where your funding will come from is filling out the Free Application for Federal Student Aid (FAFSA). You must complete this application during your senior year in high school and update it once a year during your college career. The government and schools use the FAFSA to calculate your financial aid package. You can pick up a copy from your high school guidance counselor, a college financial aid office, or by calling 800-4FED-AID. Some private and state schools require you to fill out additional financial aid forms. All the information gathered in this paperwork is used to determine the amount of money you and your family can afford to contribute towards the cost of your education—formally known as your Expected Family Contribution—and the amount of aid for which you qualify.

Financial Aid

Around the time you get offers of admission to schools, you will also receive aid packages from colleges. Based on information you have supplied to the financial aid offices in the FAFSA, schools tell you what combination of loans, work-study programs, grants, and scholarships you will receive to fund your education. Schools base their aid packages on what they consider to be your need, which is the difference between the total cost of attending a school and the amount the college

determines you and your family can contribute (based on the Expected Family Contribution just mentioned). It's not just tuition that is considered when aid packages are put together. The cost of attending school also includes room and board, books and other school-related expenses, travel costs, and personal expenses. So your aid package should take into account most of the costs you're likely to run into during school.

The bulk of student aid these days is made up of student loans. And, unfortunately, the shift in government financing of higher education is away from grants and increasingly toward loans. This places a heavy burden on students and their families who are forced to take on what can amount to huge debt loads to finance college. During the recent 1996-97 academic year, undergraduates left college with an average of about $11,500 in student loans, according to Sallie Mae, a company that buys and services student loans. By comparison, during the 1990-91 school year, students left school with an average of $8,850 in loans.

The Art of the Deal

Schools have become more open to negotiating better aid packages. So if you find that one school is offering you a better financial aid deal, don't be shy. Call up the financial aid office at other schools where you've been accepted and tell them what better aid packages are being waved under your nose. You have nothing to loose and everything to gain.

What's It Going to Cost You?

There's been a lot of press and public outcry about the rising cost of a college education. No wonder. Tuition at public four-year colleges rose more than 200 percent from 1980 to 1994, much higher than consumer prices in general. Tuition costs vary wildly, from less than $1,500 at some public, two-year colleges to well over $20,000 at some elite, private universities. According to the College Board, the average cost of tuition and fees at a private four-year college during the 1997-98 academic year was $13,664. Add the cost of room and board and the figure climbs to over $19,000.

For example, here's a breakdown from Tufts' Internet site of total expenses for a recent year at the Massachusetts school:

Tuition	$21,402
Dormitory	$3,350
Board (20 meals weekly)	$3,190
Estimated health service and student activity fees	$555
Estimated books and supplies	$600
Estimated miscellaneous expenses	$1,003
Total for year	$30,100

The numbers are enough to get your heart racing. Where are you going to get that kind of dough? Before you throw away your college applications (or your acceptance letter, if you've gotten that far), and head off to apply for a job at Burger King, read on.

While some people truly need well over $100,000 to get through college, bear in mind that it's the most elite schools that charge the highest rates. The College Board says that the majority of students at four-year schools pay less than $4,000 a year for tuition and fees, while almost 75 percent pay under $8,000 a year. That's something of a relief, but it's still not chicken feed. Let's talk about where all those dollars are going to come from.

All In the Family

Some students come from families that are able to pay all or part of their education. If you are lucky enough to fall into this group, you and your parents need to figure out what sources of personal funds to use. Many parents start saving money for their children's college education as soon as they are born. Some families pay for college costs directly out of their income, as they would living expenses like food and clothing. Besides filling out the FAFSA, you'll need to figure out your own tally of what your total costs will be so you can see what portion can be covered by your parents' available funds.

Work with your school bursar's office to determine what type of payment plan is best for you. You may, for example, be able to spread out your total annual bill into monthly installments. There is usually a charge, say $50 or so, for this kind of plan.

Be sure you and your parents read all the information that is sent to you about tuition and other payment requirements. Your eyes may glaze over when you start reading all this stuff, but it's crucial not to miss deadlines for your tuition payments. Plus, getting all the facts will prevent you from needlessly standing in lines to fix problems that could have been easily avoided.

The Family Tree

Depending upon your family situation, grandparents or other family relations can be a big source of financial help. I know people whose grandparents have set up special accounts specifically to fund their education. Tax laws dictate that individuals can give up to $10,000 a year to any number of children, grandchildren and friends before they are hit with what's known as a gift tax. A married couple can give $10,000 each, or up to $20,000 together, to any number of individuals before they have to pay the special tax. Education expenses, however, are exempt. If your grandparents or some other relatives are helping you out, they can pay tuition directly to the school, and that money won't count towards their tax-free gift ceiling. If they're in a really generous mood one day, remind your grandparents of this great, unique benefit.

Your Savings

Most of you probably have held after-school and summer jobs to earn some spending money. Some of you have even been careful to set aside this money for school. Others have socked away birthday and graduation gifts specifically to help with college. I know one student at the University of Delaware who used $650 she had saved from high school jobs working at a summer day camp, an after-school program, and a store for spending money during her freshman year. Before she started her first semester, her parents added $200 to the savings account. When I checked with her toward the end of her freshman year, she still had money left to get her through the end of the semester.

There's one drawback to having too much money in your name. When you apply for financial aid, schools can assume that you will contribute half of your income and 35 percent of your assets—money you personally have saved in bank accounts or investments. By contrast, schools assume your parents can contribute half their income and up to 5.65 percent of their assets. The lesson here isn't that you shouldn't work to contribute money towards college, it's that your parents shouldn't save too much money in your name.

Dealing with Divorce

It's not easy being a child of a divorced couple, especially when it comes to dealing with college finances. Susie, a recent college graduate, ran into a financial squeeze during her freshman year when she got caught between her parents who were in the midst of a messy divorce.

Before Susie left for college, her parents promised to finance her education—her dad would pay for 75 percent of her tuition, room, board, and books and her mom would cover the remaining 25 percent. Plus, she had worked throughout high school and summers to save money that she could use for any extra expenses. But, as an art student, Susie ran into loads of unexpected costs, from special paper she needed that cost $100 per box, to etching and other art supplies that were far more expensive than she had anticipated. Unfortunately, the money her parents had budgeted didn't go far enough, and her dad didn't understand how art supplies could cost so much. Not surprisingly, she ran through her personal savings far more quickly than she had planned.

Because Susie's parents were so busy fighting, emotions ran high. "I couldn't have a conversation with my father. I'd just burst into tears," she says. Not surprisingly, a major sore point between her parents was money, so Susie started to keep track of all her expenses in a notebook so she could show her father exactly where all the money he gave her was going.

Her parents were far too busy arguing and trying to punish each other to make sure their daughter had an easy time getting through school. Her dad didn't want to give her any more money than he'd budgeted. And her mother couldn't afford to contribute any more than she was already giving. So what did she do to cover all the extra costs she ran into? Work. More than 20 hours a week to make up the difference between what her parents had budgeted and what she was actually spending. She worked in an on-campus coffeehouse at minimum wage. She also got a job managing a darkroom on campus. The darkroom job paid good money and fit nicely with her love of photography, so that was a bonus. However, all the hours spent working put a strain on her, since she was also taking a full load of courses and volunteering for her college newspaper. But Susie was determined to enjoy the full college experience—without letting her parents divorce ruin it for her.

To try to take off some of the financial pressure, she applied for financial aid, but didn't qualify because of her father's high income. The entire time she was an undergraduate, Susie had to work long hours to make enough money to get her through the academic year.

What lesson did Susie learn? She says that if she had to go through the situation again, she would ask an adult—either a family friend or a counselor from her university—to mediate between her parents. With the help of an independent person, Susie believes the experience would have been less emotional and her parents would have been better able to separate their daughter's precarious financial situation from their personal problems.

Loans

As discussed above, students must increasingly turn to loans to help them get through school. In its simplest form, a student loan is money you borrow to pay for school. This means that at some point, you're going to have to pay it back. Keep that in mind. It's important.

Before you sign for a loan, be sure to ask:

- The interest rate.

- What fees are charged for origination and insurance. If you have a subsidized Stafford loan, for example, you'll need to pay up to 4 percent of the principal (total amount borrowed) in fees.

- Who is responsible for payments. Make sure you, your parents, and the lender know who will be held responsible for payments.

- When repayment begins.

- What, if any, grace period you are given before repayment begins.

- If the lender offers any special breaks. Some lenders, for example, reward borrowers who pay back their loans on time with a reduced interest rate or account credit.
- What, if any, penalty you are charged if you pay off the loan early.
- Information about flexible repayment plans. You may want to look for a lender that gives you different options for repaying your loan, such as paying a percentage of your gross monthly income.

Federal Loans

The best student loans are the federal Perkins and subsidized Stafford loans, which are granted based on your family's need for assistance. These loans have two big advantages: interest generally doesn't start to accrue until after you graduate and the interest rate you are charged for borrowing the money is relatively low compared to market rates.

Unfortunately, the Perkins and subsidized Stafford loans have restrictions and borrowing limits that often leave students and their families short of the total amount needed to pay for school. For those who need to borrow more or those who don't qualify for subsidized loans, the unsubsidized Stafford loan is available to students and the PLUS loan is available to parents. These are more expensive than subsidized student loans because interest charges accrue while you are in school. With the PLUS loan, parents can borrow the full cost of attending a school minus any financial aid award. The bad news is that a growing share of student loans are unsubsidized.

Private Loans

If you can't get enough from the government, a likely scenario, you're going to need to turn to other loan sources, such as private loans from banks. These loans can be much more expensive than federal student loan programs, so if you or your family intend to borrow from a private source, be sure to shop around, comparing fees, rates, and repayment terms.

Some families borrow against the equity in their home, that is the amount of money they have invested in their house. Rates on home equity loans are low relative to other sources of private loans, such as unsecured loans and credit cards. And the interest payments are often tax deductible. The danger in taking out a home equity loan is that it puts their house at risk if your parents default on the loan.

Grants and Scholarships

You don't have to be the next Rebecca Lobo (the former University of Connecticut basketball star who now plays for the WNBA) or Henry Louis Gates, Jr. (one of Harvard's star academics) to get a grant or scholarship, but you do have to work for it. Count your blessings if you get one. Grants and scholarships are gifts—they don't have to be repaid. Grants come from your school, your state, the federal government, or some combination of the three. You don't have to pay them back, but you're supposed to report and pay tax on any amount that exceeds the cost of tuition, books, and supplies. Sadly, as Ellen Frishberg, the director of Student Financial Services at Johns Hopkins points out, this means that "those who least can afford it get taxed on their financial aid dollars."

A scholarship or grant can be money that is given directly to you, or a discount a school gives you by essentially reducing its regular price tag for tuition. Morris Feldman, for example, was able to attend his first-choice school, the University of Chicago, thanks to grant money. The school took about $6,000 off the top of its regular price, making it possible for him to go there despite the fact that he'd been offered a full scholarship to attend the University of Arkansas in his home state.

Scholarships may come with strings attached. You may, for example, need to maintain certain grades or complete a particular course of study to qualify.

Finding Grants and Scholarships

Unless you're very lucky or the latest up-and-coming hockey star, you'll need to do some work to find grants and scholarships.

- Ask your school what special scholarships or grants it has for which you may be eligible.

- Check out Internet sites that offer information on scholarships (see the Appendix for some of these). If you're still in high school, ask your guidance counselor about any scholarships or grants he or she can recommend.

- Check out your local library's resources. Look for The Princeton Review's *Scholarship Advisor*.

- If you or your mom or dad is a member of any special groups, such as a church or a union, be sure to ask someone from the group if it offers any grants or scholarships. A friend of mine, for example, is part Native American and therefore qualified to receive scholarship money from a tribe to which his family could trace its roots.

Beware of Scams

In your search for free money, be wary of paying any person or business that promises to find scholarship money for you. Despite all the private sources of money that are out there, most scholarship money still comes from colleges themselves. Scams abound to entice you to turn over money to someone who promises to find scholarship and grant money for you.

How can you tell a scam operation from a legitimate service? The Federal Trade Commission, the government agency that oversees many consumer issues, offers these tipoffs to a scam scholarship search business:

- The scholarship is guaranteed.

- The search service says it will do all the work required to apply for scholarships.

- Applying for the scholarship will cost you money.

- They say, "You can't get this information anywhere else."
- You receive notification that you are a finalist for a scholarship for which you never applied.
- The search service requests your credit card or bank account number before any service is delivered.

On Her Own

Melissa Anderson is paying her own way through college. With a combination of loans, grants, and a job she found off campus, she's put together a package that will let her graduate from college with only about $5,000 in loans.

The Worcester State College junior is the youngest of five children. Just as they did with her older siblings, Melissa's parents helped pay for the first two years of school and expect her to handle the remainder of her college years. "Most of my friends are spoiled and they get everything handed to them. I like being independent. It's how I was raised," she says.

And independent she is. Melissa has an alphabet soup of student aid that helps her pay for school, from Federal Perkins and Stafford loans to Pell Grants and a Massachusetts Cash Grant. Plus, she works between 29 and 35 hours a week at a local car dealership, where she earns $10 an hour as a receptionist.

Good thing she switched from a private, two-year college to a public university. Melissa has a lot of expenses, including a $250 monthly bill to lease a 1998 Grand Am and a $190-a-month bill for her car insurance. She uses the rest of her money to pay for her other purchases and even has some left over to save. Her dorm room and meal plan are both covered in her student-aid package.

Melissa says she's never fallen behind on bills because she lacked for money. But she was so busy at the beginning of her last semester (when she was working between 40 and 60 hours a week) that she didn't have time to sit down and physically pay her bills. But that doesn't happen often.

She lived at home during her first two years of school, when she attended Becker College, and her mother hounded her to pay all bills as soon as they came in the door. She loves the money, but work can be a problem because it takes away time she'd otherwise have for her schoolwork. Still, she finished her associates degree with honors, has been able to maintain a solid GPA at Worcester State, and plans to graduate from her early childhood education program on time.

And she doesn't resent her parents for pushing her. "I've seen how the world is," she says. "And I'm glad I'm independent."

Work-Study Jobs

Be nice to the person serving a meal to you in the cafeteria and the person helping you check out your library books. That could be you. Schools provide students with jobs to help pay for their education. The money may be used for tuition or living expenses. Some work-study jobs are sponsored by schools, others by the federal government.

One advantage to a work-study job: If you work on campus, you're more likely to find an employer who understands that a student's schedule is, well, less than predictable. Graciela Ibarra of San Diego City College makes a good wage at a work-study job in her school's financial aid office. Besides giving her decent money, Graciela's boss knows that school is her priority and gives her the flexibility to switch her schedule if she has to attend class or take a test.

Charge It!

Some schools, including the University of Colorado at Denver and West Texas A&M University, let you pay by credit card. If your family has the funds to pay off the credit card balance immediately, using a card can be an easy way to funnel the money from your parent's coffers to the school. And many credit cards have special offers, such as frequent-flier airline miles, for every dollar you spend. Charging your tuition could get you a free flight to your spring break destination or home for the holidays.

Using a credit card to pay your tuition is NOT a good idea if you can't pay it all off right away; credit cards charge astronomical interest rates (as will be discussed in chapter 4), and you'll ending up owing much more than the original amount of your tuition.

If You Still Need More Money...

Depending on the cost of your school and your aid package (and let's not forget your spending habits), you may need to find a part-time job during the school year or a full-time job in the summer to help pay for school. Look in school and local newspapers for help wanted ads. Stop by your student union, the career center, or the financial aid office where there is likely to be a bulletin board full of job postings. Check out local restaurants and stores. They probably hire part-time help and are used to employing students. My friend Michael Mednick, who owns two Italian-ice stores in Chicago, hires students who are looking to work in the summer, as well as people who are willing to work flexible hours when the weather is nice.

To help pay her way through school, my friend Colleen did clerical work for an alumni publication of Cornell's business school. On Sundays, she served cookies to the people who attended church services on campus. Another friend, Anna, earned her spending money by working at a bagel store near campus. Be creative and aggressive, and you'll likely find a job that will give you a little bit of a financial cushion.

Other Ways to Pay for School

There are other routes students can take to finance the cost of an undergraduate degree from a four-year college or university.

- **Spend the first two years of school at a community college near home.** Your tuition will be cheaper and you can likely live at home, saving you the expense of renting and furnishing your own apartment. If you would like to attend a certain private college, but can't afford to pay tuition for four years, consider spending the first two years at a public university in your home state.

- **Look into Armed Forces education programs, such as ROTC scholarship programs.** Realize, however, that you'll owe the government time after you graduate.

- **Work part time and go to school part time.** If you do this, you'll need to weigh the cost of paying for your courses by the credit versus straight tuition.

It will take legwork and some creative solutions (not to mention debt) to pay your way through school. But, when all is said and done, you'll manage to pull together enough money to get through your college years.

Chapter 2

How Not to Run Out of Money

So now that you know how to get money, don't go thinking you'll have an endless supply and you can just spend, spend, spend. No matter how much money you have, you will never have an infinite supply. Even the Rockefellers have to watch their spending—you know, something like two private jets and three beach houses instead of three and four. You'll probably have more prosaic concerns, though, like eating and entertaining yourself. Possibly paying for the roof over your head. Few things are more stressful than having a $350 rent bill due when you have only $200 in the bank. So how are you going to afford your life? How do you know how much you can afford to spend?

You could just spend until the money runs out, but I don't recommend this method. It usually results in situations like not being able to eat for the last week of the month or scrambling to make a few extra bucks so you can pay the rent. You're going to need to plan how you spend your money. Yes, you're going to need to *budget*. Now, don't run away at the sight of that word—it doesn't mean hanging on to every penny for dear life and never being allowed to spend anything. Nor does it mean spending hours with your calculator figuring out where every cent went. Having a budget just means making sure you have enough money for all the necessities of life and some of the luxuries. Planning. Choosing how you will spend your money rather than waking up one day and finding it all gone. And your budget all depends on you. If you would rather spend $15 on a new CD than a good meal, go ahead. If you choose to live by yourself and have less to spend on clothes rather than split expenses with roommates, fine. As long as you plan and cover the necessities, you'll have no problem.

So how do you know what you can afford and what you'll need and want every month? How do you plan what you're going to spend when the month hasn't even started yet? Ah, an excellent question. I'm so glad you asked. This brings us to...

How Much Money Do You Have?

The first thing you need to do to set up your monthly spending plan is figure out how much money you have and how much you usually spend. No one can answer this but you. Take out a pen or pencil and flip to the worksheet on page 20. First, figure out how much money you have every month from various sources like student loans, personal savings, and your job. Fill it in on the worksheet. Include only steady sources. Don't assume that just because Uncle Eddie and Aunt Thelma sent you $100 this month, they'll be doing it every month. Only steady sources are your *income*: how much you have to spend every month.

Just How Much Do You Spend?

Now let's talk about your *expenses*: how much money you actually spend. In this chapter, we're mostly going to be talking about daily and monthly living expenses. Since tuition is often covered by loans, scholarships, or family money and paid for separately, it will be easier to figure out your monthly expenses if we leave tuition out of the equation—at least for the moment. If you pay for tuition directly out of your general budget, by all means, go ahead and add it in. Otherwise, focus on all your spending except tuition.

First figure out how much you spend on fixed expenses— those bills that come up regularly and cost roughly the same amount each time, such as rent and utilities. Fill in that part of the worksheet. Then calculate your variable expenses— purchases that come up randomly and vary in amount, such as movies, concerts, and plane tickets. Don't forget to write down your periodic expenses, which come regularly but not every month, such as holiday presents and car repairs. For categories where you don't make a purchase every month, such as a train or plane ticket home for Thanksgiving, estimate how much you spend over a one-year period and divide that number by 12 (because there are 12 months in a year, and this is a monthly spending plan). For categories where you don't spend money, leave a blank.

A month is an easy period to use for budgeting since many expenses, like rent and telephone bills, are due every 30 days or so. If you tend to figure out your money intake and outlays over a different period of time, such as a semester or a year, by all means adapt the worksheet to figure out your expenses for that period of time.

Budget Worksheet

Income Source	Monthly Amount
Scholarship:	
Grant:	
Allowance from parents:	
Savings	
Part-time or work-study job:	
Total Income:	

Housing and Food	Monthly Amount
Rent:	
Heat and electricity:	
Telephone bill:	
Groceries and/or meal plan:	
Restaurant meals and ordering take-out:	
Total Housing and Food Expenses:	

School Supplies	Monthly Amount
Books:	
Notebooks, computer paper, etc.:	
Copy center bill:	
Newspaper and magazine subscriptions:	
Total School Supply Expenses:	

Budget Worksheet

Personal Care	Monthly Amount
Laundry and dry cleaning:	
Health insurance co-payments and prescriptions:	
Toothpaste, shampoo, etc.:	
Haircut:	
Gifts:	
Total Personal Care Expenses:	

Transportation	Monthly Amount
Car payment:	
Insurance:	
Gas and tolls:	
Repairs:	
Bus or subway fare:	
Taxi fare:	
Plane or train ticket home:	
Total Transportation Expenses:	

Entertainment	Monthly Amount
Concert tickets:	
Movie tickets:	
Health club membership:	
Cable television bill:	
Parties:	
Total Entertainment Expenses:	

Total of All Expenses:	

Does it Balance?

Once you've completed the worksheet, compare your expenses to the amount of money you have to spend. No, no, no, they're not hopelessly far apart. If you find you're spending too much, look for areas where you can cut back. We'll get into more detail on trimming expenses later in the chapter. First we need to make sure you've accounted for all your expenses so we have a fair and accurate picture of how much money you're spending.

Does This Cover Everything?

No doubt there are items we left off the list or items you don't purchase every month or even every semester. Many financial planners—people who have expertise and get paid to dole out advice on money—suggest you carry around a notebook that you can use as a budget diary. Write down all your expenses for a period of time, such as a week or a month. Everything. Even a cup of coffee. Notice all the items you may have forgotten to include in your formal monthly spending plan. These incidental purchases, such as a cup of coffee

Sample Spending Plan for a Net Monthly Income of $1,000

Housing
(20-35%) _____

Food
(15-30%) _____

Personal Debt
(10-20%) _____

Transportation
(6-20%)_____

Utilities
(4-7%)_____

Clothing
(3-10%)_____

Personal Care
(2-4%)_____

Insurance
(4-6%)_____

Health
(2-8%)_____

Misc. Items
(1-4%)_____

Savings
(5-9%)_____

(Source: Consumer Credit Counseling Service of the Gulf Coast Area.)

here or a candy bar there, add up. If you purchase lunch five days a week, you could be spending $80 a month more than you realized. Buy a newspaper and a cup of coffee on your way to class every day and you could be spending approximately $6 a week that you didn't know you were spending. That comes to $24 a month, or almost $300 a year. Really? Yes. You mean I'm spending the same amount on newspapers and coffee that I could spend on a plane ticket? Yes. But if you like your daily newspaper and coffee, forgo the plane ticket. If you'd rather go to Mazatlan for spring break, then you might want to change your spending habits. Which brings us to the next section—how you can change the way you spend money (if you want to).

How Much Do You Really Need?

It's the rare and lucky person who doesn't need more money than he or she has. Still, most of us can probably get by with what we have. How much you need depends on what your necessities are and where you live. It's more expensive to go to college in San Francisco or Miami than it is in Des Moines or Champagne-Urbana. The rent is higher, food costs are likely more, even a ticket to the movies will probably cost you more than in smaller towns. Ask yourself what your necessities are. Obviously, you need a place to live and food to eat. If you go to school in Anchorage, you've got to budget ample money for heat. You must also buy books for your courses. And you'll need notebooks, an occasional haircut, and some clothes.

The important thing is to be realistic. You don't need to eat out three times a week. And you don't need to rent an apartment with a whirlpool. "A lot of students come in with a standard of living or an expectation of a standard of living that they don't necessarily need to maintain," says Steve Van Ess, director of the Office of Student Financial Services at the University of Wisconsin at Madison. Don't be one of them. Give up the whirlpool and cell phone.

What Can You Cut Out?

When money's tight for me I like to run through a checklist of items I can hold off on purchasing. Ask yourself: Do I really need a haircut this week? Must I eat out when I could cook some pasta at home? For college students, eating out and entertainment are big expenses. "Food [eating out] is a real gobbler of that loose money," says Merriott Terry, executive vice president of operations at the Consumer Credit Counseling Service of the Gulf Coast Area, an organization that helps people deal with debt and money management. And, do you need to go to two concerts this month? Wouldn't one be enough?

Betsy Koerner, a student at Northwestern, says her school's dining halls close at 7 p.m. But she and her friends don't usually go to sleep before 2 a.m. Sound familiar? That leaves a lot of hours for them to get hungry. All the pizza they order can become a big expense.

Besides cutting back on those midnight snacks, there are other places to look for savings. Here are a few ideas:

- Read the newspaper and your favorite magazines in the library instead of purchasing your own copies.

- Make coffee at home instead of buying it from a cafe. Get yourself one of those portable coffee mugs and carry it to class with you.

- Stock up on snack food that doesn't cost a lot of money, such as bulk nuts and dried fruit from the grocery store. Besides costing less, you'll save on the delivery charge or tip.

- Pack your lunch a few days a week instead of always buying it in the cafeteria, a deli, or a restaurant.

- Make long-distance phone calls at night when the rates are usually cheaper.

- Wait until clothing goes on sale before making a necessary purchase, such as a winter coat.

- Buy used books at the campus store.

- If you own a car, consider whether you really need one or see if there are ways you can carpool and get other people to share some of your expenses.
- Watch out for weekend bingeing.

"In college you like to have fun," says Kim Votava, a manager at the Consumer Credit Counseling Service of Southern New York in Manhattan. No kidding; that's a big part of college life. But because of your limited budget, you're going to have to learn to balance fun with the need to spend wisely. In chapter 7, we'll cover strategies for smart shopping and getting the best deal whatever you're buying. In the meantime, when it comes to your budget, carefully consider what your necessities are.

Control Your Spending

If you love to spend money, you'll need to come up with ways to avoid spending when you don't have enough cash. Peg Downey, a financial planner in Silver Spring, Maryland, suggests another use for the spending diary mentioned above. Use the notebook you carry to write down purchases you are interested in making. Include a description of the item, the store where you see it, and the price. Then walk out of the store. "Reconsider it," she says of the purchase. If you decide you can afford it and still want to make the purchase after careful consideration, then buy it later.

Downey also recommends shopping with a friend, someone who will help you think twice about purchases. These strategies should help you cut down on what is known as impulse buying—picking up something on the spot that you didn't necessarily need or plan to purchase. Your friend should be able to convince you that purchasing that rhinestone-studded jacket that is in vogue would be an expenditure you'd regret.

Ask Yourself a Few Questions

The Consumer Credit Counseling Service suggests you pose these questions to yourself before you make a purchase:

- Do I need it?
- Do I have to have it today?
- What will happen if I don't buy it?
- How have I managed this long without it?

If your parents are supplying you with money for living and other general expenses, you'll still need to be careful about your spending or your parents may pull the plug. Dara, a student at Hobart and William Smith Colleges, recently overspent the monthly amount her parents allocate for her extras. It wasn't the first time she spent too much. So when she turned to her parents for a cash infusion, they decided it was time she learn to budget better—and they turned down her request, forcing her to cut back on new purchases.

Cutting the Cord

Emily Slowe is determined to wean herself off her parents' money. When we spoke with her, the University of Massachusetts at Amherst sophomore was getting $200 a month from her parents for spending money. But she recently started earning about $40 a week by working as a waitress and expects that, as her paychecks become more regular, her parents will cut down their monthly contribution. "I don't really like taking their money," she says. "I feel guilty."

While her parents will continue to pay tuition, Emily says she feels uncomfortable having them pay for her other expenses because her dad is retired and her mom is about to retire. "It's their money. It's not my money." But they all agree it's a good idea for her parents to pay her tuition: They can afford it, and no one in the family wants Emily to graduate with a pile of debt.

Last summer, she worked three jobs to bolster her earnings—working as a lifeguard, running a swimming program, and working at a day care center. This summer, she plans to work as a nanny, as well as tend bar or waitress. While she's at school, Emily tries to limit her spending to about $20 a week for groceries and $20 a week for entertainment. She's cut out buying clothes and other impulse purchases.

Emily says she's surprised by how much money it takes to run a household, and by "how much the little things add up." And while she's careful not to rack up credit card debt, she does have a card that she uses occasionally so she can build a credit history. "My brother didn't want a credit card when he was in college and then when he went to graduate school, he couldn't get his own card because he hadn't built a credit history."

When You've Spent Too Much

It'll happen. Despite our excellent advice, sometimes you'll overspend. It's a pain, but it's not the end of the world.

Just what should you do when you've spent too much? Cut back. Just as when you eat too much at a holiday meal and have to cut back your food intake for a while, when you spend too much money you need to cut back. Cook more meals at home. Rent a video instead of going to the movies. Borrow a book from the library instead of spending $25 on the latest novel from your favorite author.

You just need some time to recoup. We call these periods "the austerity mode." When we've spent a lot of money, intentionally or unintentionally, we go into austerity mode—no new clothes, no concerts, no fancy meals at great restaurants. Stay in this mindset until your bills are paid up and you have a cushion back in your bank account.

"I had a lot of money in my bank account and basically had no reason not to spend it," says Ben Bloom of his first semester at Boston University. Ben got to college and found lots of temptations that led him to spend much more money than he did at home—from CDs to meals outside his prepaid plan. Ben was lucky. He realized pretty quickly that he was spending too much money and changed his habits. Ben says, "I don't spend any money that I don't have to spend. After the first month, everyone realized how strict their budgets were."

During her first month at Hobart and William Smith Colleges, Mary Maloney and her roommate were spending $30 to $50 a week on groceries. Problem was, they had a meal plan both their parents had already paid for. And they were plowing through their money at a fairly rapid clip. So they decided to go to the dining hall.

Like Ben and Mary, a lot of students get to school and spend more than they should. Or they have occasional months when they blow their budget because a favorite band comes to campus and they just have to go, or they want to buy a new sweater to beat the winter blues. Or they can't resist the temptation to join their friends in Cancun for spring break. Probably the most tempting time to spend beyond your budget is when you're a first-semester freshman or at the start of any fall semester. If you've been working at a summer job or just cashed your student loan check, your bank account is looking far richer than it normally does. "I kind of went a little overboard the first month, so I cut back a little bit. Money goes really fast here," Mary says. It'll go fast wherever you're going to school, too. Watch your spending.

What If Your Friends Can Spend More Than You Can?

Find new friends. No, seriously, you need to do what's best for you. Maybe you can spend as much as they can when you go out one night, but can suggest something cheaper, like renting a video and buying pretzels another night.

Say you have only $50 a month to spend on food, but your roommate likes to buy exotic fruits and vegetables, imported beer, and bakery goods. The two of you need to sit down and set up a household budget—the amount of money you designate to spend jointly on certain items. First, look at your fixed costs, such as rent and utilities, and split them fairly. Then, based on how much money you each have to spend, set up maximum amounts you can afford to and are willing to spend as a household for things like food, cleaning supplies, and parties. Agree that you'll you'll individually pick up the amount you each spend over your joint budget.

It works the other way around, too. Just because you've built money into your budget to go to a concert once a month doesn't mean all your friends can afford the luxury. Talk. Compromise. And above all, know what you can do. Don't do it just because everybody else is doing it, and that goes for a lot besides spending money.

Living Within Your Means

Remember, setting a budget is not about depriving yourself of pleasures. It's about being responsible for matching how much money you take in with how much money you spend. Your monthly spending plan is flexible. When you have extra money from a summer job or when Uncle Eddie and Aunt Thelma throw a few bucks your way, you can spend a little more on fun stuff. And if during the academic year you find your budget isn't working, say you've allocated too little money for food, you can and should readjust it. In that case, you'd look for areas where you could spend less money so you could devote more cash to buying groceries or paying for more points on your school meal plan. It's very satisfying to know that you'll have money for everything you need in any given month. So develop a monthly savings plan. And stick to it.

Learning Financial Independence

Mary Beth Giancarlo says the hard lessons she's learning about managing money today will help her after she graduates from school. "I'm really learning what I should be spending my money on," says the sophomore at Hobart and William Smith Colleges. "I think that by the time I get out of school, I'll be a pro."

Before she left home for her freshman year, Mary Beth's parents told her that she'd have to pay for her all of her books and spending money during college. That wasn't a problem her first year of school when she had money saved up from high school jobs working as a lifeguard, teaching swimming, baby-sitting, and doing office work. At the end of the year, she even had $400 left over. But then, last summer, "I didn't get out and get a job right away." That left her with only about $600 in earnings from her summer job to make it through the school year, far less than she needed. By the time winter term was winding down, Mary Beth worried that she wasn't going to be able to buy books for the upcoming spring semester.

"I know that if I had zero dollars and I complained a lot to them, my parents would dish out some money. But they wouldn't be too happy about it," Mary Beth says. "If I were really in financial trouble, they'd pitch in." Instead of turning to her parents, she says she'll see what books she can get from the library and she'll speak with her professors about which ones she really needs to purchase.

Mary Beth says she's determined to learn from her mistakes—like the time she racked up $80 in bounced check fees because she didn't keep track of what checks she'd written. To improve her habits, Mary Beth is trying to keep careful track of all the purchases she makes, as well as how much money she has coming to her in each paycheck so she can better ration it. "Things are more expensive than I thought. Money slips away before you know it."

Chapter $3

Banking 101

Until now, you may or may not have had a checking or savings account where you deposited birthday gifts or money you earned from an after-school job. Now, you'll definitely need an account you can rely on as you write rent checks, settle tuition bills, and send off those payments to the telephone company. The world of banking can be confusing, with a slew of institutions offering a host of accounts with different fees and requirements about how much money you must keep on deposit to avoid extra charges.

A 1996 survey by *Consumer Reports*, for example, found that fees on accounts can vary by $40 a month within the same area. At the same time, banks are trying to entice their customers into other products and services, from student and car loans to investment products. This chapter will give you a handle on the best ways to find and use a bank, as well as give you the knowledge you need to fight back against unwanted or excessive charges.

Lucky for you, banks often have special deals for college students. They want to get your business and loyalty early on so that when your big bucks start to roll in, you'll continue doing business with them. Take advantage while you can—many of us who are already out of school are left to pay up the wazoo in bank fees.

Why bother with a bank account? You need one. Without a bank account, your life would be a hassle. With an account you can:

- Keep your money in a safe place.
- Get cash when you need it.
- Write checks for rent, books, your phone bill, etc.
- Keep track of how much money you have to spend.
- Keep track of how much you've already spent.

Choosing a Bank

One of the first things you'll need to do just before or after you get to school is choose a bank where you'll set up an account. As you may have noticed, some banks will advertise for your business in your student newspaper or set up a booth on campus during orientation. Some schools even include information about local banks in orientation packets. Trevor Hughes of Boston University, for example, says you can show up on campus for your freshman year and already have an account open. Remember, as long as there is more than one institution near campus, you have a choice about where you bank. You can choose one of the institutions that comes looking for you or do some shopping around on your own. Trevor saw an ad for a local bank offering free checking and no-fee ATM withdrawals, so he opened an account there.

Banking institutions come in various shapes and sizes. Commercial banks tend to be larger banks that have corporate as well as individual (retail) customers. Savings banks focus primarily on individuals, offering checking and savings accounts, auto loans, and mortgages. Credit unions are nonprofit financial institutions set up to serve the financial needs of one particular group, such as employees of a particular business. Credit unions typically offer lower-cost alternatives to consumers than do large commercial banks, with better rates on loans and more liberal requirements for no-fee checking accounts.

The Home Court Advantage

So much banking these days is being done by telephone and computer that you don't necessarily need your bank to have a branch near campus. Also, as the banking industry consolidates, a growing number of institutions like Bank of America, Key Bank, Citibank, and First Union have a presence across one state or across an entire region of the country. If that's the case with a bank near home that also has branches near your school, you can easily keep your account with the same institution. One advantage of keeping your account at home is that your parents can easily deposit money for you. (We should all be so lucky.) When I was in college, I did my banking at Marine Midland, which had branches near my parent's house and near school. This worked well when I

Stats and Facts

Percent of large banks that offer special student or youth accounts: 49

Median balance required for free checking at large banks: $500

Average monthly fee banks charge consumers who fall below minimum balance requirement: $6.60

Average bank charge for a bounced check: $15.71

Average number of monthly transactions handled by tellers at large banks: 2,747

(Source: Federal Reserve; American Bankers Association)

needed my dad to co-sign an auto loan I took out just before graduation. I was able to talk to a loan officer at a branch in Ithaca, New York, while my dad was able to take care of the bulk of the paperwork and provide his much-needed and much-appreciated signature. Plus, using a bank near home made it easy to set up a system where my parents deposited a set amount of spending money into my account at the same time every month. Also, if you're living at home in the summer, you can use the same account.

If you do decide to keep your bank account near home, make sure there are ATMs near school that you can use. Banks belong to various networks of teller machines, such as Cirrus (operated by MasterCard) and Plus (operated by Visa). Your ATM card can generally be used in any machine in the U.S. and still others overseas. Later, we'll talk about what fees you may rack up using ATMs outside of your bank's *proprietary network* of machines—those machines operated by and carrying the name of your bank.

The Campus Choice

If you go to an out-of-town school and decide to bank away from your hometown, you can find a bank near campus. Call a few local branches and see what special offers, if any, they have for students. Again, many institutions will come looking for you so you may not have to do too much legwork. But if you don't like what's pitched to you, keep looking. There's a good chance there's another bank near your dorm or apartment. A local bank may even have one or more branches or ATMs set up on campus. Mike Barnes at Arizona State, for example, told us he chose to set up an account with Bank of America because it operates ATMs in his school's student union and around campus.

Choosing an Account

Your basic account choices are checking and savings accounts. Checking accounts let you deposit money and access your funds via checks, ATMs, and increasingly, computers. Savings accounts are meant to give you a place where you can stash away funds for a longer period. With a savings account, you don't have check-writing privileges, but you do earn interest (however little). A checking account will likely be enough for you. But if you're the type of person who spends every penny that's at his or her disposal, you may want to open a savings account linked to your checking account. You can use the account to stash away funds until they're needed. Then you can transfer money to your checking account.

Student Accounts

A good number of banks offer special accounts designed specifically for students. Look for one. They usually require a lower minimum balance, or amount of money you need to keep on deposit at the bank to avoid a monthly account maintenance fee.

First Union, for example, has an account called College Express Checking that waives the bank's usual minimum balance requirement and monthly maintenance charge for students who have a paycheck deposited directly into their account and do all their banking through First Union ATMs. The catch: the bank charges $8 each month you choose to handle any of your transactions with a teller. By contrast, First Union's Personal Checking account requires a balance of $750 to avoid the monthly fee of $12.50. Deposit Guaranty in Mississippi offers its GuarantyFirst checking account free to people between the ages of 15 and 21. Account holders get free checking no matter what their balance size and they aren't charged for the first 25 transactions they make each month.

Some student accounts have restrictions on the number of transactions you can make each month and the location where you can make them. Non-student accounts that have limits on both usage and cost are known as basic or no-frills accounts. Almost 90 percent of large banks and 84 percent of medium-sized banks offer these, according to the American Bankers Association. Basic accounts are generally geared to low-income or low-transaction consumers, so if a bank doesn't have a student account, ask about basic accounts. Don't forget to compare student accounts to regular options at each bank you shop just to ensure that you are indeed getting a good deal.

Check!

Before you open any account, consider what you need and want from a bank. Use the start of a semester to make sure your bank is serving your needs—that it offers the best combination of convenience, service, and affordability. Consider:

- Are there ATMs near your dorm, your work-study job, and your significant other's place? What, if anything, are you charged for using them?

- Approximately how many transactions will you make each month? As we said above, some student and no-frills accounts limit the number of checks you can write and the number of ATM withdrawals you can make. How much will you be charged if you go over the limit?

- Will you need to use ATMs other than those that belong to your bank, say when you visit your grandmother or go home for the summer? How much will you be charged?

- Do you want a debit card (which you'll read about later in the chapter)? Are you charged a monthly or yearly fee for it?

- Do you want your bank to help you with other loans for a car, say, or a credit card? If so, make sure your bank offers these in a form that is attractive.

Setting Up an Account

When you actually do open an account, make sure you have what you need:

- Your Social Security number.

- Money to deposit (in the form of cash, a check, or a money order).
- Identification (a driver's license or passport).
- Your signature (which presumably comes with you wherever you go).

You Are the Customer

That means you have control. If you don't like something your bank does, like charging you too high an interest rate on your credit card or being too restrictive about the number of transactions you can make each month for free, you can always look for a better deal elsewhere.

If you switch banks, make sure you've closed all your accounts properly. You don't want to be racking up interest payments or fees you don't deserve. Even if you've closed your account, be sure to open any mail you get from your old bank. I recently closed one bank account only to start getting notices that the account was overdrawn. I was being charged a fee because I was below its required minimum. Needless to say, there was no money left in the account because it had already been moved to another bank. I had to call the bank's customer service department many times before the bank stopped billing me.

Also, if you close your account and have any bills—such as student loan payments—paid automatically from that account, be sure to notify the merchant of the switch.

The Cash Dispenser

Ah, access to money. Ever been starving, but have no cash to pay for a late-night snack?

Automatic teller machines have changed the face of banking. Thanks to the electronic machines that let you deposit money, check your balance, and withdraw cash at any hour, you may never step in a bank lobby again. Since the first ATM was installed more than 20 years ago, the number of machines in the U.S. alone has climbed to over 120,000.

Now that consumers are hooked on ATMs, banks are

making them more expensive to use. The median charge in 1996 for bank customers who used a machine that didn't belong to their bank was $1. Some banks charge you for using the ATM every time you fall below your minimum balance requirement. And now a growing number of banks are charging non-customers who use their machines. This surcharge means you can be charged twice for one ATM transaction—once by your bank for not using its own machine and another time by the bank that owns the ATM you use. A 1997 article in *The New York Times* pointed out that when all the fees were added together, ATM users in New York were typically paying an average of $2.50 to withdraw cash from machines.

Watch for change in this area. As of this writing, a handful of states had already prohibited banks in their state from slapping on surcharges. And some politicians were clambering to outlaw them nationally or, at the very least, require banks to warn customers at the time of a transaction that they'll get a fee slapped on if they complete the withdrawal.

Still, banks want you to use ATMs. It's cheaper for them to buy and operate the machines than to employ tellers who otherwise would be processing your transactions. As a result, some banks are setting up accounts that encourage consumers to use the ATMs exclusively. People who had a low-cost Versatel account at Bank of America in 1997, for example, had to cough up $2 every time they used a teller for a transactions that could have been done at an ATM.

ATMs and Your Monthly Spending

Some people try to use ATM withdrawals to budget their monthly allowance, figuring if they only take out $10 at a time they can't spend too much money. While it's not a smart idea to walk around with bundles of cash in your pocket, you also don't want to have to make a trip to the ATM every day. I was living in New York City for at least six months before I admitted to myself that $40 withdrawn from the cash machine didn't last very long.

"ATMs are lethal [to your budget] because you just keep going and going," says Betsy Koerner of Northwestern. It's easy to take out too much money and forget that you have.

You need to be careful to budget your trips so you don't blow your monthly allocation by withdrawing too much money too soon. Also, you don't want to rack up excess fees by going to the ATM too often. Chances are you won't be using your ATM withdrawals to bankroll any trips to Las Vegas, but you should know that banks limit the amount of cash you can withdraw each day. At Citibank, for example, customers are limited to $1,000 a day at Citibank ATMs and around $500 at other banks' machines.

Be sure to request a receipt from the machine and mark down every ATM transaction. You'll need the information to keep tabs on how much money is in your account.

Watch Out

When you walk up to an ATM, chances are you're there to take out money. Be careful. Robbers can see the opportunity to take advantage of the situation. Just in case you haven't thought of them yet, here are a few common sense safety tips:

- Try to go to the cash machine during the day.
- Try to go to a machine in a high-traffic area.
- Be aware of your surroundings.
- If you have to go at night, consider asking a friend to make the trip with you.

If Your Card Is Lost or Stolen

Report it immediately to your bank. The amount of money you can be held liable for varies based on how quickly you report that your ATM card is missing. Report it within two business days, and you'll be responsible for a maximum of $50 if someone uses your card without your permission. Wait any longer, and you can be liable for much more.

Balancing Your Account

Your balance is the amount of money you have available in your account. Because banks can make mistakes and because you should know how much money you have, you're going to need to balance your checkbook register (the book where you record your account activity, including every deposit, check, and withdrawal). Balancing your account is the practice of matching what your checkbook register says you should have with the bank's monthly statement of what you actually do have on deposit. You may want to use a computer program, such as Quicken, to balance your account and handle other parts of your personal finances.

Remember when I suggested that you keep the receipts you get at the ATM? To balance your account, you'll need to compare all your deposits of cash and checks against the bank's listing of this activity. And you'll need to compare each ATM withdrawal, check you've written, and debit card transaction. Also check the list of fees printed on your monthly bank statement and make sure it is correct and that you've subtracted that amount from your balance.

What if I Spend More Than I Have?

Needless to say, you always want to make sure you have enough money in your account to cover any checks you write, otherwise you'll bounce them. To protect yourself against writing a rubber check, look into overdraft protection—a line of credit on your checking account that lets you borrow money in cases where you spend more than is on deposit in your account.

When you write a check for an amount greater than your balance, you go into overdraft. Medium and large banks commonly have a minimum of $300 to $500 and a maximum of $5000 to $10,000 protection, according to the American Bankers Association. Of course, you have to pay for the privilege, so check what interest rate you will be charged for any money you borrow and ask what fees are associated with the service. Banks generally charge an annual fee for overdraft protection.

Be careful to use overdraft protection only for emergencies. I spoke with a student who, at one point, owed almost $500 on her checking account. She had tapped the credit line at the same time she was revolving more and more money on her credit cards. Recognizing her problem, she's since cut the overdraft amount in half, but is using her entire paycheck to pay off the debt. As you'll see in Chapter 5, you know you are in trouble if you are starting to borrow from one source to pay off another, such as needing to borrow cash from your checking account to pay your credit card bills.

Working the Late Shift

Brad Graeber fits in his schoolwork between his paying jobs. He works about 30 hours a week in the advertising department of the *College Station Eagle* in College Station, Texas. He's the visual arts editor of his college paper. And he does freelance graphic work for the local government. Not surprisingly, Brad pulls a lot of all-nighters.

All of Brad's hard work pays off. When he moves to Dallas in the fall for an advertising job, he won't have any debt. He covers his tuition at Texas A&M University, as well as all of his expenses like rent and food. And he's steered clear of credit card abuse his entire time in school. It took his older brother several years after college to pay off the $20,000 he accumulated on his credit cards. And he has a friend who's already graduated and has been paying off $13,000 on his credit cards for more than a year. "I saw that as a warning sign," he says. "Avoiding plastic—that's part of the protection plan."

But Brad hasn't had such luck with his bank account. "I try to keep track as best I can, but sometimes something slips through," he says. Some of Brad's "slips" have included writing one check too close to depositing money in his account, and not factoring into his balance all of his bounced check fees. Say he bounces a $5 check for a hamburger and gets hit with a $20 fee from his bank; he may not know about the fee until he receives his statement the following month. And because of the fee, he has less money in his account than he calculated. So when he writes another check, thinking he has the funds to cover it, he too often bounces another check. "It goes downhill from there," he says.

When money is tight, he and his roommate turn down

the heat or cut down on their food bill. "We have a cabinet full of ramen noodles," he says. Plus, he's learned to love apples because he can buy them cheaply in bulk. The biggest crunch, Graeber says, is rent because, no matter how he slices it, he must cough up $270 a month to keep the roof over his head.

Debit Cards

Your ATM card is a debit card—every time you use it, money is taken directly out of your bank account. Besides using your ATM at the cash machine, you can often use it to make purchases at a store. Banks also issue two other types of debit cards. These look like credit cards and are accepted by many merchants. They usually carry your bank's name along with a logo from Visa or MasterCard. Some of these cards also double as your bank ATM card.

With debit cards, your money is taken directly and almost immediately out of your account. Debit cards have a few drawbacks. The money is automatically deducted from your checking account, so you lose the grace period that credit cards offer by giving you free use of the money before it is actually taken from your account. And you may be charged a monthly or yearly fee for using the card.

College Bank Cards

Some universities are linking up with local banks to offer multipurpose campus/ATM cards. First Chicago NBD, for example, issues these at Northwestern and Indiana University-Bloomington. The cards serve as student identification cards, act as your entrance card to campus dining halls, and let you store money that can be used in school vending machines.

These multipurpose cards can also double as your bank ATM card (if you decide to open an account with the bank). Northwestern and Indiana students who choose to bank with First Chicago NBD, for example, can use their student ID card as their ATM card if they have an account. Their card is linked to First Chicago's Self Service Accounts, which have no minimum balance requirement and no monthly fees as long as all transactions are done electronically.

Gotcha: Fees to Watch Out For

Banks charge for almost everything. You probably know that banks sock you if you bounce a check, request a money order, or stop payment on a check you've written. But now you're being charged for everything from asking the bank to make a copy of an old check to depositing someone else's check that bounces. The *Consumer Reports* story I mentioned earlier says the magazine identified 100 different fees banks charge consumers.

There is no limit to what banks can charge for services, but they do have to let their customers know 30 days before they raise a price. That's why it's so important to read the inserts banks send with monthly statements. They give you the heads up about changes in fees, account terms, and special offers.

Bank personnel have a lot of flexibility to waive certain fees. If you are ever charged for a service or item you feel is unfair, by all means call the bank and ask someone there to remove the fee. Banks are out to please their best customers. As a student, you may not qualify for the greatest number of breaks, but it never hurts to ask. There's a lot of competition out there for your business, and banks know they can lose your account.

"A student dollar is just as strong as anyone else's," says Eric Lundberg from the University of Wisconsin at Madison. He once racked up $116 in fees when he bounced six checks. He had deposited one check into his account. Assuming the check was fine, he wrote six others to pay various bills. Problem was, the check he deposited bounced so he didn't have enough money in his account to cover the checks he wrote. He spoke with a manager at the bank and explained the situation. In the end, he was able to get the $116 in fees knocked down to $22.

Other Bank Services

Banks want you to turn to them for a host of services besides checking and savings accounts. They sell credit cards, home and auto loans, certificates of deposit, money market accounts, insurance products, and mutual funds. For now, you'll likely just need a bank to supply you with a checking account and credit card. You may even have your student loan with one.

Here are some other offerings you'll run across:

- **Certificates of deposit.** Commonly known as CDs, these are time-based deposits. You give the bank a set amount of money for a specified period, usually from one month to five years. When the CD matures, you get back your money plus interest. Interest rates vary based on market conditions, but they are higher than what your money would earn in a savings account. There is usually a hefty penalty if you withdraw your money early.

- **Money market accounts.** Money market accounts invest their assets in liquid securities, meaning cash investments that mature within 60 days or so. Rates fluctuate with the market and are typically higher than what's paid on savings accounts but lower than the rate on money market mutual funds. Money market accounts are insured; money market mutual funds are not.

- **NOW accounts.** NOW stands for negotiated order of withdrawal. These accounts are basically interest-bearing checking accounts. They usually have high fees associated if you dip below the minimum balance requirement. These days, NOW accounts pay such a low level of interest that they're not worth your attention.

The Future of Banking

For years, banks have been touting the next wave of banking. It took years to get off the ground, but finally, with the growth of computers and our increasing comfort with ATMs, more of our banking needs can be taken care of outside a branch. A growing number of banks now let customers transfer money between accounts, pay bills, and direct investments from their computers. Consumers can also take care of almost any transaction over the phone that they could in a branch. Some banks, like Chase and Citibank, have their own PC banking systems. A number of banks let customers access their bank accounts through Intuit's *Quicken* and Microsoft's *Money* personal finance programs. And some have electronic bill paying services that let you pay bills by phone or have recurring bills, such as a car or student loan payment, made automatically. Not all banks have all of these services, and prices vary.

You may be hit with a charge of several dollars a month for the privilege of paying your bills electronically or doing your banking by computer. A spring 1997 report on the Bank Rate Monitor Internet site of PC banking fees showed a wide range. Provident Bank in Maryland, for example, charged $7.99 a month for accounts with balances under $3,500. Citibank, Corestates, and Security First Network Bank were free.

Banks are also beefing up virtual branches on the Internet, where we'll increasingly be able to apply for loans or check our account balances in cyberspace. Many banks already have extensive Internet sites that provide information on their offerings and ATM locations, as well as general consumer information. Some even have sections of their Web site devoted to student finances.

A handful of banks are also starting to test smart cards—plastic cards that let you store money and information on a chip embedded in the plastic. Merchants equipped to take smart cards debit the purchase amount directly from the amount you've "stored" on the card. They work like prepaid phone cards.

It's going to be you and your friends who help bring a revolution in banking. You are the first consumers who, *en masse*, know how to use computers and will demand easy access to your financial assets.

Chapter 4

The World of Plastic

You may have noticed that you have little or no income.
Yet it seems that everyone and his mother wants to give
you a credit card. Why? Because the credit card companies
know that you will see a fast rise in your income once you
graduate. That means you'll likely be buying and spending
a lot more money than you do now, and, simply put, credit
card companies want a piece of the action. Credit card
companies realize they can build brand loyalty. Who
wouldn't love the company that gave them their first piece
of plastic? Plus, if they lend you money to help you buy all
those goodies you need while in college, they'll earn oodles
in interest. Assuming, that is, you can't afford to pay off all
your bills immediately.

Remember, you are not being offered a credit card because of your great personality. Lenders know you need money and that you are willing to pay a price for it. And they know that you have a pretty good chance of earning a decent salary once you graduate. College graduates earn about 60 percent more than workers who have only a high school degree.

You've got to be careful with credit cards: You can get in over your head quickly. But don't worry, this book is here to guide you using plastic, as in all other money matters.

What is a Credit Card?

A credit card is a piece of plastic that lets you borrow money from a bank, retail store, or other lender. You can pay back the money you spend in full each month or spread out payments over a period of time. Whatever amount you borrow and repay is immediately available for you to borrow again. Lenders limit the total amount you can spend to what is called your credit limit. Credit cards for students typically have a credit limit of $500 to $2,500. I'm not an advocate of overcharging. But I do want to say that if you need more credit, ask for it. When Trevor Hughes of Boston University, whom we mentioned earlier, was going to London for a semester abroad, he asked his credit card company to increase his credit limit so he would be protected in case he needed access to more money for emergencies. That was a smart move.

Free Money? Sounds Great!

Not quite free. Because credit cards are loans, you have to pay interest on the money you borrow. The amount of interest credit card companies, also known as issuers, charge is called the annual percentage rate, or APR. This interest charge is where lenders make the bulk of their money and where you have to be careful not to get yourself into trouble. At this writing, the average interest rate on credit cards is about 18 percent, meaning you would pay $18 a year in interest for every $100 you borrow. That's not cheap. Cards issued by retail stores often have even higher interest rates. And most credit cards have interest rates that vary based on the current economic situation. So when general interest rates rise, you can bet that the rate on your credit card won't be far behind.

There are other ways that credit card companies cash in on your need to borrow. A recent solicitation for Discover Card, for example, points out that the interest rate on its card jumps to 22.15 percent for users who do not make two consecutive payments on time.

If it's Not Free Money, Why Have a Credit Card?

Despite the potential for card companies to capitalize on your poverty, there are several reasons why it's important to have a card:

- **Emergencies.** This is the number one reason to have a credit card in your wallet. Say one of your parents gets sick and you need to fly home unexpectedly. With a card, you can call an airline and instantly buy a ticket. Chances are you won't run into such a scenario, but you really wouldn't want to face one without a credit card.

When Eric Lundberg, a student at the University of Wisconsin at Madison, was in Florida for one of his winter breaks he got a serious sinus infection and missed his flight back to school. He used his credit card to pay for a visit to a doctor, the medicine he needed to get better, and a replacement plane ticket for his return trip. The total bill came to about $1,000—all of which he got back when he submitted his medical bills to his health insurance company and talked Continental into paying for the replacement plane ticket after he explained why he missed his flight.

- **Convenience.** Credit cards allow you to make necessary purchases—such as books and that snazzy jacket—without carrying large amounts of cash in your wallet.

- **Credit history.** Credit cards let you establish a record of your ability to manage your finances; this record is known as your credit report. Having a good credit report, which means a good credit history, will be important when you graduate from school and need to take out an auto loan, for instance, or have a credit check done before you can rent a new apartment. Consider a credit history like your permanent record, only unlike your academic record, it tracks your financial moves.

How Do You Get a Card?

Chances are you don't have to try too hard to get a credit card. The card companies will find you before you need to look for them. When I was in college, I had a credit card offer at the bottom of every bag I took out of the campus store. You probably do too. Then there's your mailbox. "Every time I go to my mailbox there's a credit card offer," says Devin Gordon of Duke University. When my brother Gary was in college, he ran a business signing up people at Princeton for various credit cards. As you've probably seen on your campus, there are several companies that operate these businesses today, setting up booths to sign you up for one or more cards. Many card companies even offer enticements. Michael Chant, a student at the University of Wisconsin at Madison, signed up for an additional credit card because he was thirsty. Students operating a booth to sign up other students for credit cards were giving away soda in exchange for a completed credit card application, so he went for it.

But there are some far better deals than free soda out there. Recent applications for AT&T's Universal MasterCard were touting vouchers for low student airfares on USAirways. American Express was offering low fares on Continental and six hours of free long distance phone service on MCI. Before signing up for a card just to receive some reward, consider the offer. It may pay to sign up for a card that gives you substantial travel discounts. But it doesn't pay to sign up for several cards at once just to get a gift worth a few bucks. You can run into problems if you have too much credit at your disposal.

In addition to the risk of running up balances on many credit cards that you may not be able to pay off, there are serious implications for your credit rating. Each time you acquire a credit card, the total amount of credit available to you increases and is passed on to credit reporting agencies. The more credit you have, the more difficult it will be for you to acquire additional credit. Why is this important? The one-time 10-percent discount you received at a retail store in exchange for signing up for their credit card won't seem very important to you when you apply for a car loan and you're turned down because you have too much credit at your disposal. Lenders see this and realize one shopping spree could send you into major debt.

Plus every time you apply for a card, your credit records are accessed, causing an "inquiry" into your credit status. Too many inquiries can often result in you being turned down for a future credit card that you really need or want.

One good way to avoid the "too much credit" problem is to cancel those cards that you acquired just to get a free soda or a 10-percent discount. But the only way to avoid too many inquiries is to stop applying for every card that is put in front of you. There are a number of credit card companies, including Citibank, MBNA, and First USA that make a big push in the college market. Your campus newspaper will probably carry advertisements trying to entice you to a particular offering or a particular type of card.

If no card company comes calling, you can apply for a card from the bank where you have a checking account or any other issuer that offers a product you like. Credit cards are issued in the name of almost everyone, from your local bank to the nearest department store to your favorite environmental group. Whatever card you sign up for, be sure you know what annual fee and interest rate you will be charged.

Most people have a credit card that carries the name of Visa or MasterCard. Both are associations of banks that issue credit cards. Besides Visa and MasterCard, the bulk of other cards used are issued by American Express and Discover. Lenders issue regular and gold cards. Gold cards typically have higher credit limits and more perks than a standard card. As a student, you probably won't qualify for a gold card since they are generally reserved for people who make at least $30,000 a year. A growing number of companies now offer platinum cards to their wealthiest and best customers—these have even higher credit limits, but not many additional perks you'd find useful.

You can also apply for a card that has a low-interest rate or one that comes with special perks, such as giving you one frequent flier point for every dollar you charge on the card. However, you may not qualify for these special perk cards because they are largely reserved for the card companies' best customers. Ilana Silver of the University of Delaware wanted a Citibank credit card that would get her miles on American Airlines, so she had her parents co-sign for the card. With their income, she was able to qualify.

It's good to know (whether you have gainful employment or not) where to find the low-rate and best credit cards. Some newspapers and magazines, including *Money*, occasionally run lists of the current best credit card deals. RAM Research has a list of low-rate cards and provides good general information about credit cards (see the appendix for information about them).

Lehigh University surveyed its students about credit card use. While the survey wasn't scientific, it did have some interesting results. According to a brochure put out by the school:

- 72 percent of the students who responded have two or more credit cards.

- 13 percent had balances over $2,000.

- 26 percent have missed payments.

- 58 percent pay their balance in full each month; 12.5 percent pay the minimum amount due.

- 80 percent use earnings or savings to pay the bill.

Other Ways to Get a Card

If you are having problems getting a card or don't want the full responsibility of maintaining a credit card account yourself, consider asking your parents to co-sign with you. That way you share responsibility for the bills. Also, you can ask your parents to order an extra card on their account in your name. You won't build a credit history or get the same sense of responsibility for budgeting as you do by maintaining your own card, but you will have a credit card that you can use for emergencies.

Finally, some lenders now issue secured cards for consumers who do not qualify for a regular credit card because they have a bad credit history or no credit history at all. Lenders require you to deposit money with them. If you default on the loan, the lender takes the money out of your account to pay the balance. In essence, the credit card is secured by the money you leave on deposit. As with all cards, know what annual fee and interest rate you will be charged for using a secured card.

Carrying a Balance

More than half the consumers who use a credit card revolve or carry over a balance—the amount of money they owe—from one month to the next. Don't follow their lead. Try to pay your bill in full every month. Otherwise, you can find yourself in a pile of debt. Let's say that in the first month you have a card you charge $300 the first day of the month. You make no more purchases all month and get a statement that says you owe $300 on the account. On the 15th of the next month, you send in a check for $100 to your credit card company and, that day, go out and charge another $150. If you charge nothing else all month, you would owe about $5 in interest. If that doesn't seem like much money, consider the math and remember that interest continues to accrue every month. Borrowing $350 for one year at 18 percent costs about $60 in interest. If you pay only the minimum amount due every month—usually two to three percent of the total balance—it would take years to pay off the $350 and, by then, you'd have racked up ridiculous interest charges.

At the time of this writing, the average balance per person was $1,627, according to RAM Research, a Maryland-based company that tracks credit cards. On your income, it would take an awfully long time to pay off that amount. Card account holders with average balances are paying about $375 in interest charges each year, according to RAM. In total, Americans had more than $520 billion outstanding on their credit cards as of August 1997!

Don't add to the problem. I can't stress enough the importance of paying your credit card balance in full each month. Here's the trap: If you don't pay off your balance in full, interest starts to accrue on the amount of money unpaid, also known as the amount of money outstanding. And if you keep charging new purchases, you will find yourself immediately paying interest on your new purchases. There's a temptation with your first credit card to buy anything you want. Resist it. If you have questions about how much you can afford to charge or need strategies to avoid overspending, refer to the chapter on budgeting and remember that eventually you have to pay real money for anything you purchase with your credit card.

The Credit Counselor's Perspective

Kent Johnson is a credit counselor with Consumer Credit of Des Moines, a nonprofit organization that offers consumers advice about dealing with debt and money matters. Six times a month, he sets up shop at the Iowa State University Credit Union, where one out of every four or five people he counsels is a college student.

"When I was a college student, you couldn't get a credit card to save your life," says 34-year-old Johnson. Now, he often sees students with $3,000 and $4,000 credit lines who are piled knee-deep in debt. The students he sees, he says, charge designer clothes, stereos for their cars, you name it. The day before I spoke with him, he had counseled a student who didn't qualify for student loans because his parents made too much money, so "the credit cards acted as his student loan."

Johnson helps the students who turn to him get a handle on their outstanding loans and figure out how best to pay them off. He routinely helps students set up a budget and a debt repayment plan, where they make regular, monthly payments. His office works directly with lenders to try to get interest rates on outstanding loans lowered. And he also speaks with lenders, when necessary, about accepting smaller monthly payments when a student is serious about paying off his debt, but can't afford the payments the way they are currently structured.

Lenders back these nonprofit credit counseling services and routinely work with offices to make it easier for clients to pay off their loans. In the end, it's more beneficial for these companies to take less money from borrowers in the form of lower interest payments than it is for them to see cardholders walk away from their loans altogether by defaulting.

Some cases are extreme. Johnson sometimes finds himself suggesting that a student cut back on the number of courses he is taking in order to work more hours and earn enough money pay off outstanding debts. One recent college graduate he spoke with has $27,000 in loans. With an annual income of about $20,000, Johnson says this client doesn't make enough to make a dent in his debt. Johnson suggested he get a second job or he might find himself needing to take the extreme step of filing for personal bankruptcy.

Johnson makes clear that he is not anti-loan. "I don't see a crime in borrowing money. I just think it's gotten way out of hand. Every day, I see at least one person, maybe two, with at least $30,000 on credit cards." He points out that with this debt burden, someone would need to pay $450 a month in interest payments alone.

That's a lot of hours working at a job that pays minimum wage.

Using Your Card to Your Advantage

If you pay off your balance in full every month, you get to use your lender's money for free for several weeks. Say you buy a pair of jeans and several CDs on the 14th of January. If your card company mails your bill to you on the 28th of the month, you won't have to send them your payment until sometime in February. So you basically get the jeans and the CDs for an interest-free loan of about four weeks. The period before your bill is due is known as the grace period. If you carry a balance, you lose the grace period on any new purchases.

Still, many students need to revolve credit from time to time. You may have a cash flow problem, or you may have overspent one month. The important thing to do is to cut back on new purchases when you start to gather debt and to start paying off the amount you owe. If you owe money on more than one credit card, first pay down the card that carries the highest interest rate. And always call your credit card issuer and ask if it will lower the interest rate it is charging you. In the past several years, competition has led credit card companies to be a lot more generous to customers.

If you're not happy with the deal the issuer offers you or if you don't like any of the terms, you can always get a new credit card and cancel your old one (that is, after you've made sure you paid off all the money you owe or transferred the balance to another credit card). You'll find that issuers may offer you enticements to stay.

Charge Cards

Lenders also issue charge cards, such as the American Express and Diners Club cards. These are different from credit cards in that you are required to pay the bill in full every month. These cards come with a fairly steep annual fee. The Diners Club card, for example, costs $80 a year. (American Express also issues "free" Optima cards, which are no-fee credit cards that you can use to revolve a balance). If being able to carry a balance on a credit card is too much of a temptation for you, you may want to get a charge card instead of a credit card. Also, American Express and Diners Club cards offer a bunch of travel benefits.

Earning Perks

These days it seems everyone is putting their name on a credit card—American Airlines, Blockbuster Video, Shell gasoline. When retail stores or organizations link up with a lender to issue a Visa or MasterCard in their name, they issue what is called a co-branded credit card. With each charge, you earn credit toward the product of your choice, such as an airplane ticket or free gasoline. Many of these cards come with a cost. They often have a very high interest rate and an annual fee. Credit cards linked to airline frequent flier programs, for example, carry annual fees that range from $35 to $60 or more. But most cards today have no annual fee.

In the case of frequent flier cards, you'll be spending approximately $50 a year for the privilege of earning one mile for every $1 you put on the card. If you charge $200 a month, it would take you over 10 years to earn enough miles to get a free, round-trip ticket for travel within the

United States. By that time, you'll have already spent $500 in annual fees alone. Avoid these cards unless you spend enough to make the annual fee worthwhile.

For students, there is one case when it definitely pays to have one of these cards. As we said in chapter 1, some colleges and universities allow you to pay your tuition with a credit card. If you go to an expensive private college, you don't want to put $18,000 on your card if you can't pay it off immediately. But if you have money in a bank or investment account that you are going to use for your tuition bill, you should consider putting the payment on a credit card linked to a frequent flier program or some other program. If you don't qualify for one of these cards, you may want to encourage your parents to get one. As we said in chapter 1, there's no reason one of you shouldn't get a free plane ticket for the price of a year's tuition!

The Protections of Plastic

Credit cards carry a good amount of protection for consumers. If you have a dispute with a merchant about merchandise or a service that costs more than $50 and was bought within your home state or within 100 miles of your address, you can ask the credit card company to take the charge off your account. That's called charge-back protection, and you can use it when a merchant doesn't deliver a product or service that you bought. Some cards also insure purchases against theft or damage and pay for the collision damage waiver insurance when you rent a car (though I realize it can be hard for college students who are under 25 to find a car rental company that will rent to them). Federal law also has strict provisions for how card companies must respond to you if there are errors in your bill.

If you need to charge back a purchase or notify your issuer of a problem on your bill:

- Call your credit card company.

- Put the complaint in writing (usually you can do this by filling out a special section on the back of your monthly statement).

- Send the complaint to the special address for billing disputes. The address will often be listed on your bill. If not, call the issuer to get the proper address.

- If there is a mistake on your bill, notify your issuer within 60 days of the charge appearing on your credit card statement.

When You Have a Problem

When you get a new credit card, always write down the account number as well as the toll-free customer service number that is listed on the back of the card. Keep that information in a safe place or give it to your parents to hold. If your card is lost or stolen, call the customer service number immediately. By law, you are liable for only $50 of any unauthorized purchases made with your card. Card companies often won't even make you pay that amount. Also, call the customer service number if you see any charges on your monthly bill that don't look familiar. In 1996, I found two wrong charges on bills. Both charges were taken off my bill after I contested them.

Watch Out! Don't Believe Everything You Read

Credit card companies mail out a few billion offers for cards to consumers each year, so don't be too flattered when you get their solicitations in the mail. Instead, be skeptical. Here's what to look for in the fine print:

- **Teaser rate.** Many card offers come with unbelievably low interest rates. These rates are typically teaser rates to attract you to the card. Generally, they rise within a few months. As of this writing, the prime rate that banks charge their best corporate customers was 8.50 percent. Any rate that is at or lower than the prime rate is likely a teaser rate. Some teaser rates apply only to balances you transfer to the card, while you'd pay a higher rate on any new balances.

- **Freebies.** Don't be tricked into signing up for a card just because its annual fee is zero. Remember, most cards don't have an annual fee. Read the fine print to make sure a no-fee card doesn't add a fee in subsequent years.

- **Sky's the limit.** The line of credit highlighted on your offer is the top amount a lender will give you, not a promise of how much credit you'll actually receive.

- **Graceland.** You want a card that has a grace period, a number of days you have before you must pay your credit card bill. Otherwise interest payments will start to accrue as soon as you make a purchase.

- **Yet more fees.** Card companies will charge you for a host of things, from paying your bill late to spending more money than your credit limit allows. There can also be fees associated with using your credit card to take out a cash advance from an ATM. The rate you're charged will probably be higher than the rate you pay on purchases. Now, some card companies have started to add some outrageous fees, including a penalty fee if you cancel your account. Watch out for cards that charge late fees. Pay some bills ten days late and you'll be asked to pay not only the interest but also an additional fee of $20 or so. Finally, some companies will cancel your account if you always pay on time because you are not racking up interest and they are losing money on your account.

Thanks, But No Thanks

Some lenders send out offers, often around the holidays, trying to entice you to skip a payment on your credit card or bank line of credit. The only thing you should skip, however, is the offer itself. The offers are enticements to get you to rack up even more debt. Every time you skip a payment, you lengthen the time it will take you to pay off your debt. You increase the amount of interest you will have to pay for borrowing the money. Plus, some lenders charge you for the privilege, adding a fee if you skip a payment.

Nuts and Bolts

- Don't be tempted to get too many cards. As a student, you should be fine with just one. As your credit needs get more sophisticated, you may want two cards—one that is attached to a frequent flier or other perk program and one low-rate card you can use if you need to buy something that you can't afford to pay off right away.

- You'll receive a monthly bill or statement that lists the month's transactions, the total balance due, the minimum amount due (that is, the minimum amount you are required to pay towards your balance without incurring a penalty fee) and the date by which you must make your payment to the credit card company. If you pay only the minimum amount due on your monthly bill, interest will be added to the balance left unpaid. Also, as we said, if you don't pay the bill in full, you lose the grace period and interest starts to accrue immediately on any new purchases you make. Remember, you only get a grace period and free use of your credit card company's money if you pay off your balance in full every month.

- Credit card companies use one of several ways to calculate interest charges, including the average daily balance of your account or the average monthly balance. When you are choosing a card, make sure you know what method the card company uses. That can be as important as knowing the annual percentage rate of the card. Avoid cards that use so-called two–cycle billing, because it can be more costly if you carry a balance.

- Stay up-to-date. Be sure to read the inserts your issuer sends with monthly statements. That's where you'll find, often in fine print, notice that fees are being increased or added to your account.

- If you cut up your credit card, you still haven't closed your account. You'll need to call the lender to do that.

- Make sure your credit card company knows where to find you. If your bill normally goes to your college address, but you move or leave town for the summer, make sure you let the card company know where it should send your bill.

Chapter $5

Payback Time

If you've already filled out the budget worksheet in chapter 2, you have a good sense of how many regular and not-so-regular expenses you now have. From paying your monthly telephone bill to making credit card payments, you probably feel like you have an awful lot of companies lined up to receive your money. And, in fact, you probably do. This chapter will help you handle the mechanics of paying bills. We'll cover the importance of paying bills on time and options for physically getting your money where it's due.

We'll also cover strategies for managing any debt you may acquire. Let's be honest. It's the rare and independently wealthy person who doesn't borrow some money at least once in his life. Face it: It's hard to get through college without borrowing at least a little.

Debt is a serious topic. It may seem like nothing to you to rack up some money on your credit card or blow off an occasional payment. But don't forget, you have to pay off the money you borrow. If not now, then someday. Plus, lenders can put any negative information on your credit report, where it will stay for seven years. Let's forget student loans for a while. Student loan debt is an animal unto itself, deserving of its own chapter (see chapter 10). One big difference to keep in mind between student loan debt and other debt is that student loans are like an investment. You borrow money to go to school so you can get a better paying and more interesting job when you graduate. Credit card debt isn't the same. There's no investment value to concert tickets. So, in this chapter, we want to focus on credit card debt and any other loans you take out to get through school, from borrowing an extra $100 from your roommate for rent to going into overdraft on your bank account.

Set Up a Routine

When it comes to paying bills—monthly or one time statements from companies with whom you've done business—you'll need to find a routine that helps you get your payments in on time. I'm pretty task-oriented, and I actually like to pay bills. The very act of going through a pile of mail and getting current on various accounts makes me feel like I've accomplished something, so I catch up on bills about once every week or two.

Other people let their bills pile up for a month or so before they sit down with their checkbook. Still others let their bills slide and pay them whenever they get around to it or just plain blow off the whole enterprise. We don't recommend either of the last two methods. Companies report delinquent payments to the credit reporting agencies that compile your credit report. You can also be charged a late fee. Time Warner Cable in New York, for example, charges $5 for accounts that are past due. Most importantly, if you don't pay your bills within a certain period of time, the company to which you owe money can cut you off and, depending upon which bill you haven't paid, you can lose your electricity, your phone service, your credit card, even your apartment.

What's Due

Take a few minutes to look over the budget worksheet from chapter 2 and figure out what bills you have to pay monthly. Chances are the list includes:

- Rent
- Telephone
- Utilities (electricity, water, etc.)
- Credit card
- Cable

Then figure out what bills are due less frequently, say twice a year, or only occasionally, such as tuition, doctor bills, auto insurance, and magazine subscriptions.

Keeping It All Straight

Set up a system that works for you in terms of helping you keep tabs on what bills you have to pay and when you have to pay them. You can use separate folders for each bill, say one manila folder for your telephone bill, one for your credit card account, and one for your rent statements. Then you can pick a regular time every two to four weeks to go through each folder. Or you can keep a pile of current bills on your desk or hall table where they'll be in your line of vision until you pay them. After you've sent in the payment, you can file the bills in folders by category or year, say all bills from 1998. One strategy I've used when I've been tight for cash and couldn't afford to send in the payments early is marking my calendar to pay a specific bill four days before it's due. Whatever method you pick, make sure it works for you.

Be sure to read the due date on each bill and get your payments in on time. If you don't, you can start to rack up the late fees we just mentioned, and you may also get hit with interest charges. With credit cards, for example, interest payments kick in on outstanding balances and all new purchases once you pass the due date.

Signing on the Dotted Line

The conventional way to pay bills is to sit down with your checkbook and write a check for each and every bill. If you do this, mark down in your checkbook register the amount you've paid and the date when you wrote your check. You'll need this information in case a company claims it hasn't received your payment. You'll also need the information to balance your checkbook.

Some people who don't have checking accounts use money orders, which are check-like substitutes issued by the post office and private companies. But this can be costly. Right now, U.S. postal money orders cost 85 cents each. So if you have more than a few bills to pay each month, you'll be down several dollars in money order fees.

Most bills require you to put a stamp on the envelope. I know it seems obvious, but if you forget to place the proper postage on the mail, you're going to miss the payment deadline. And since it's easy to let outgoing mail pile up near the door, be sure to mail the bill in time for it to arrive by its due date.

Going Electronic

About a year ago, I started doing a lot of my banking on line. My bank lets me check my balances, transfer money between accounts, and pay bills so I now use my computer to pay my phone, utility, and cable bills. Since my bank also issues my credit card, I use my electronic bill paying service to transfer money from my checking account into my credit card account. My landlord isn't set up to receive electronic payments, so it would take my bank about seven days to get my payment in. I figure it's just as easy to pay the bill with an old-fashioned check, so I mail one myself.

Like other on-line banking programs, mine gives me the option to set up recurring payments that every month are sent for a specified amount on a specified date. I don't use the recurring payments (and I suggest you don't either) because I like to check each monthly bill for accuracy. Once you have a regular bill, like a student loan or home mortgage that is due in the same amount on the same day each month, recurring payments may make sense. Otherwise, I think it's best to keep control over who and how much you pay.

My bank, Citibank, is one of several banks that provide electronic bill paying for free. But in general, while paying bills electronically may save you the hassle of licking stamps, it won't necessarily save you money. As of this writing, most banks charge between $5 and $10 a month for an electronic bill paying service. You can also use a program like CheckFree or a personal finance program like Quicken to pay your bills. If you do use one of these, you'll need to sign up and pay for the service. And in the future? We should soon start to see some companies deliver our bills via the computer instead of snail mail.

Keeping Control

Some companies ask for permission to dip into your bank account to pay off your monthly bill. I think this is a bad idea since it's safest when only you have access to your account. As I said above, I like to check each bill for accuracy, and the only way to do that is to review each one before it's paid. Plus, if you have a dispute with a company, it's much harder to withhold money to fight a company that has access to your bank account.

Sharing Responsibility

If you have a roommate or several housemates, you'll have to coordinate bill paying for all the shared expenses in your home. Some phone companies offer a service that lets you punch in a code and designate who gets charged for each call. Other than that, however, you'll be left alone to divvy up the remaining bills.

Julie Black of Vanderbilt says she and her two suitemates sit down to reconcile the money each has laid out once they start forgetting who has paid for what purchases. "Money shuffling, we do that a lot," she says. "We're trying to keep up with it now as it comes along so we don't get so confused."

Josh Kinsler, a junior at the University of Virginia, shares a university-owned, off-campus apartment with a few friends. Since they all have different schedules, "we all buy our own food and do our own thing," he says. Electricity is included in their rent, and their campus phone service bills them each individually for their calls. Last year, before the school switched to the phone service that billed them separately, they would each underline their personal calls on the monthly phone bill. One roommate "was always on top of things" and would tell everyone when they needed to pay a bill.

If your name is listed as the responsible party on a bill, say your cable service is under your name, you're the one who will be held liable for payments. To avoid tension, make sure you and your roommates discuss who is responsible for contributing to and actually paying each and every bill that comes in.

Record Keeping

Just how long do you need to keep your old telephone bill? Will you ever look at your old credit card statement again? Here's a rundown of what you can toss in the garbage and what you should hold on to.

Toss these after you've paid the bill and seen proof (the next bill, a canceled check, etc.) that your payment has been credited to your account:

- Utility bill

- Phone bill

- Magazine subscription bill, doctor's bill (unless you need it for insurance purposes), etc.

- Cable

- Rent statement

Keep these a year or longer:

- Bank statements

Don't confuse keeping old bills with general record keeping. You need to hold on to information about warranties, insurance policies, and other important documents that have information that is necessary and useful for the long term. And if you mistakenly throw away a bill that you need, call the company and ask if it can issue a replacement copy.

Cutting Your Bills

Now that you realize you're going to have to pay bills, there are a few ways to cut how much you actually have to shell out each month. I talked about some of them in chapter 2, but here are some more.

Turn off the Lights

You probably can hear the words coming from your parent's mouth. But it's true: Turning off the lights cuts your electricity bill and satisfies your environmentalist urges all at the same time. I live in New York, where the summers can be brutally hot. When I turn on the air conditioner in June, my electricity bill soars. To keep the bills as reasonable as possible, I make sure I turn off the air conditioner when I leave the apartment. And if I'm going to be in the living room for any period of time, I turn off the air conditioner in the bedroom.

Utility companies often offer free home energy audits to help you figure out how to make your home more energy efficient, a move that can save natural resources and money. If you live off campus and think your house could use some improvements, say the apartment doesn't retain heat in the winter, consider calling your local utility company to ask for an audit. Chances are you rent your apartment or house, so you may need to ask the building's owner to request the energy audit.

Ron Reisman, a spokesman for Elizabethtown Gas in New Jersey, offers these tips:

- When you're not using them, turn off lights, appliances, computers, etc.

- Keep the thermostat set at a comfortable level, say 68 or 70 degrees (and consider wearing a sweater indoors in the winter to help cut the heating bill).

- Clean the refrigerator (especially the coils) and defrost the freezer.

Some utility companies have a budget billing plan that lets you spread your monthly payments into equal installments. This helps smooth out the bigger bills consumers usually have in the summer and winter from extra cooling and heating needs.

It's common for a utility company to require you to give it a security deposit, money to guarantee you can cover your bills. You get the money back when you move. Some companies will waive their security deposit requirement if you get a letter from your previous utility company that says you paid your bills on time. If you have to leave a deposit, you may be able to get the money back before you move out if you pay your bills on time for a respectable period of time.

Cutting the Cable Connection

No doubt about it, it's nice to have cable. Who doesn't like to veg out in front of VH-1 or ESPN? But cable can be expensive. You can easily pay more than $30 a month for cable service, which adds up to well over $350 a year. On a student's budget, that's a real luxury.

When my friends Karen and Yoram were both still in school (she was at New York University and he was at the Fashion Institute of Technology), they got rid of their cable. "We were having a budget crunch," Karen says. So they looked over a list of all their expenses and realized they couldn't cut their rent or electricity. And they didn't want to trim the amount they spent on their telephone calls. So they got rid of their $25-a-month cable. Says Karen: "It gave us that feeling of satisfaction that we were actually going to save money on something."

Jessica Glasser says she only recently signed up for cable service. She's a sports fan and loves to watch baseball and hockey. But she waited until she had extra cash from her first job out of George Washington University in Washington, D.C. before she signed up for the cable service that would pipe ESPN into her home.

If you want cable service or need it to get good reception, sign up for basic service and then decide whether you can afford to pay for premium service.

Debt and Borrowing

There are going to be times when you truly need to borrow money. Say your car breaks down and you've spent an extra $150 getting it fixed so you don't have any cash left to pay for groceries. By all means, you shouldn't starve. So the next time you go grocery shopping, you may have to go into overdraft on your checking account or use your credit card. Sometimes you might be making a large purchase, such as a car you need for school or work, and you need a loan. (We'll discuss shopping for a car in chapter 7.) All is well and good if you borrow a reasonable amount and are responsible about paying it off.

Signs That You're In Over Your Head

How do you know when you've crossed the line and borrowed too much? Here are some of the warning signs that you are in trouble:

- You regularly spend more than your income or budget.

- You regularly put small purchases, like groceries and gas, on credit cards because you don't have cash available.

- You owe more money than you now have or are likely to have in the near future.

- Month after month, you can pay only the minimum payment required on your credit card.

- You can't afford the minimum payment required on your credit card.

- You are borrowing from one source to pay off another.

- Credit collectors call about one or more accounts.

Piling on Debt

"I don't budget myself at all and I spend on impulse." These words can be disastrous. And they have spelled trouble for college student Nicole Girard. The University of Massachusetts at Amherst student got her first credit card soon after she started school. She waited one month after she received it and then went on a holiday spending spree. She charged hundreds of dollars in purchases. Add in food she'd order in to her dorm room and trips to the mall, and Nicole was soon at the outer limits of her $500 credit limit. She called her credit card company, which gladly raised her limit by $100. That only gave her the chance to get herself further into debt.

Because she couldn't afford to pay it off, Nicole started revolving her balance and accumulating interest on her credit card. And while she tried to make payments on time, she'd sometimes mail in her check late, which added a $25 late fee to her account each time she missed the due date. After she ran into other billing problems when the company didn't seem to get her payments on time, she closed the account. But that didn't erase the debt. Even though she doesn't have use of the card, Nicole is still paying off an outstanding balance of $530 that she has left on it.

That's not all. Nicole signed up for another credit card and owes another $800 she accumulated by charging a plane ticket, books, and other expenses. How does she feel about her pile of credit card debt? "It does stress me out a lot. I feel like I can't manage my own finances."

Indeed, Nicole does have a problem with her spending and budgeting. To dig herself out of debt, she now tries to pay for any new purchases she makes with cash or a debit card, where her money will be immediately taken out of her checking account. She orders out for food a lot less than she used to, pays cash for any clothes she buys, and tries to cut down on her impulse purchases. Says Nicole: "I realized I had to stop spending on my credit cards when I maxed out."

What To Do When Trouble Strikes

As I wrote in the chapter on budgeting, the first step to taking control of your finances when you've spent too much is to stop spending. This won't help reduce the amount you owe, to be sure, but it will keep you from getting further in the hole.

Sports fan Jessica Glasser racked up credit card debt only once or twice when she was at George Washington University. But that was more than enough for her. "My parents brought me up not to charge more than I could afford to pay," she says. So during the five months or so it once took her to pay off the debt, she stopped eating out and buying music. "I started cutting back on the wants instead of the needs."

Like Jessica, if your debt problems aren't too serious and you feel confident that the amount you owe is manageable and can be paid off pretty quickly, here are some of the steps you can take to wipe out the debt:

- **Stop spending on things you don't need.**

- **Stop paying for purchases with your credit card.**
  Once you owe money on your credit card, buying more will only increase your debt. Plus, any new charges you make start to accrue interest immediately.

- **If need be, cut up your credit card.** Remember, however, that you haven't closed the account until you notify the lender that you want it closed.

- **Ask the lender to lower the interest rate it charges you.**

- **Use savings to pay off debt.** There's no reason to earn interest of 2.5 percent in a savings account if you're paying 18 percent interest on a credit card. Use the savings to pay off your plastic, and you'll be ahead almost 16 percentage points.

- **Work more hours at your current job or, if you don't have one, get a job.**

- **Consider asking your parents for an interest-free loan.**

- **If you owe money on more than one credit card, be sure to pay off the balance on the higher-rate card first.** If you use this strategy, don't forget to keep paying at least the minimum amount due on your other accounts.

- **If you are revolving a balance on a high-rate credit card, apply for a credit card with a low interest rate that lets you transfer an existing balance from another account.** Then move the existing balance from your high-rate card to your new, cheaper card.

- **Pay as much above the minimum payment on your credit cards as possible.** Otherwise, you'll spread out repayment for an incredibly long time and rack up even more interest charges.

Pick Up the Phone

Perhaps the most important part of handling your own finances is knowing when to ask for help. If you've gotten in too deep with credit cards and still can't manage your debt after following the steps listed above, call your creditor. That is, call the phone number listed on the back of your credit card or call your bank if you're in overdraft, and ask to speak to a customer service representative.

Explain your problem. Ask if the creditor will consider waiving any penalty fees you may have racked up and extending your payment period. Be sure you mention that you have every intention of paying off the loan and that you just need some short-term help. It's cheaper for creditors to get most of the money back than to get none of it if you are pushed into default—that is, when you abandon a loan because you can't pay it off. So there's a good chance they'll be willing to work with you.

If You Can't Handle it Alone: Taking Care of Serious Debt

Don't be afraid to ask for outside help. If your problem becomes so serious that you can't afford to pay the minimum amount due each month or you are stressed about the amount of money you owe, consider calling a counseling service. Your campus student affairs center, financial aid office, or other university group may offer budget counseling services. Texas Southern University in Houston, for example, has a student peer credit counseling service where students can talk to another student about credit questions or problems.

You can also contact the National Foundation for Consumer Credit, a nonprofit organization that offers credit counseling services nationwide. Call 800-388-2227 to be referred to an office near you. Counselors at these offices help you set up a budget and, if necessary, they work directly with lenders to set up a repayment plan.

In New York City, Consumer Credit Counseling Service is helping Jennifer, a 23-year-old undergraduate, pay off the $8,500 she owes on three credit cards. "I would come home to five calls a day from creditors calling me about giving them money," says Jennifer. Jennifer's problem was shopping. She bought clothes and luggage and had her hair cut at the fanciest salons in Manhattan. "The more I bought, the less I thought about it," she says. "At one point, the minimum payments were up to $300. That's my whole paycheck."

A customer service representative at one of her credit card companies told her about Consumer Credit Counseling Service. But it wasn't until she heard about the organization again—this time in a magazine article about a woman who was obsessed with shopping—that she set up an appointment. Jennifer's budget counselor negotiated with her creditors to get lower interest rates and reduced penalty fees. In exchange, Jennifer recently started paying $186 a month towards her debt. She'll need to make payments for five years before she is debt free.

Like Jennifer, Rachel Aydt turned to CCCS for help. Rachel, who went to the State University of New York at Albany, put herself through college by working as a waitress and taking out student loans. She had to use her credit cards to buy textbooks, and since she was an English major she sometimes spent $200 on books for one course alone. By the time she graduated, moved to Manhattan, and had to live on a low starting salary, she was using her credit card at the grocery store. Soon her debt became too hard to handle and creditors came after her. "My phones were ringing off the hook. It was a really depressing situation. My personal finances were out of control."

Rachel had $6,000 in credit card debt when she called Consumer Credit Counseling. A counselor there was able to negotiate and get the interest rate on her Citibank Visa lowered to about 8 percent from 21 percent. "I'm still living check-to-check and it's still difficult. But I'm actually paying off my debt now," says Rachel, who pays $350 a month toward her outstanding balances. She'll be debt free within five years.

Not All Credit Counselors Are Alike

There are a lot of businesses out there that want to take advantage of your debt problems. You've probably seen their ads in the newspaper or their commercials on television. Some companies advertise that they can clean up negative credit reports, others that they will intervene with your creditors to get rid of your problems.

Not so fast. Be wary of anyone or any business that makes promises that sound too good to be true. After all, how can anyone clean up your credit report if you've legitimately skipped payments or defaulted on a loan? Also watch out for anyone who requires you to make a payment before he delivers on his promise. Stick with nonprofit or campus credit counselors and you should be fine.

If you are still considering using a for-profit debt or credit repair shop, check them out with a local Better Business Bureau office or your local consumer protection agency, whose number can be found in the blue pages of your phone book.

Legal Protections

The law protects you from what debt collectors can and cannot do. A collector may not contact you at unreasonable times or places, such as before 8 a.m. or after 9 p.m., unless you agree, and he may not contact you at work if he knows your employer does not approve. You can stop a debt collector from contacting you if you write a letter to the collection agency telling it to stop. You will still owe money, but the agency may only contact you to say there will be no more contact or that it intends to take a specific action against you.

Staying Clean

If you get into a routine of paying your bills on time, you should be able to avoid problems with debt. But if you do run into trouble, don't run away from it. Take control, and you'll see that you can handle your bills responsibly.

Chapter 6

A Roof Over Your Head

Now that curfews and home-cooked meals are a thing of the past, you have to make some decisions about where to live. And while you may prefer to live in the Taj Mahal, you'll need to get a grip on reality. Just what can you afford? And if your parents aren't there to fix the plumbing when it breaks, where do you find a plunger? What do you do with one anyway?

This chapter will walk you through the process of deciding where to live, whether you're thinking of living on campus or off. It will cover strategies for looking for an apartment, tips and traps of signing a lease, suggestions for physically setting up your home with telephone service, heat, pots and pans, and general information you need to make a home out of a room in a residence hall or a private apartment.

On Campus or Off?

You may not have a choice. First-year students at Bowdoin College in Maine, for example, are required to live on campus. Yale and Harvard are famous for the residential colleges where underclass students live. Whether you have to or not, you may decide you want to spend part of your university years on campus. There are a lot of advantages to on-campus life, from being close to classes to having all of your needs taken care of. If you live in a residence hall, for example, you probably won't need to clean the bathroom or vacuum the living room. And the laundry room, when you absolutely, positively can't go another day without clean clothes, is probably just steps away. Some schools have facilities with nearby gyms and game rooms—a fine distraction when you're supposed to be spending your free time studying.

Schools usually have a range of housing options: single-sex floors; substance-free residence halls; special language houses; where students who are interested in particular languages, such as French or Chinese, live; town houses; residence halls for transfer students; international houses; you name it. When I checked, the latest figure available for the average annual cost of a student room on campus was just over $2,000. The average annual cost of board (food) was just under $2,000. Schools typically send out housing information, including options and prices, to incoming freshman and transfer students. Your school—or one you're interested in—may also have housing information on its web site.

In general, campus leases typically run for ten months. That's great if you don't want to pay a full calendar year's rent when you're only going to use the room for the academic year. But it can be a hassle if you're planning to stay at school year round. After her freshman year at Vanderbilt University, Julie Black stayed on campus to spend the summer working for the school's conference office. There was a gap between the date by which she had to be out of her freshman room and the time her summer residence opened. So she had to move all of her stuff to her boyfriend's place. Then to her summer home. And then, when there was another gap between when that lease expired and her sophomore-year room was available, she had to divide her stuff among friends' places before she could move it all into her new residence hall. What a hassle. If you're planning to stay at school during a winter or summer break, check with the housing office to see how you can minimize any hassles.

Read through all the school's housing information. Think about which part of campus you like best. Do you want a roommate or not? What amenities do you need? Would you rather be near a dining hall, for example, or your 8 am biology lab? Or would you rather live off-campus?

Making the Decision

If you're a freshman or sophomore who has the freedom to decide whether to live on campus or off (or if you're an upperclass student who is no longer required to live on campus), ask yourself a series of questions to help you figure out where you'd like to live. For some students that may mean living at home. When he decided to go to the University of Alaska in Anchorage, Ben Roberts knew living at home would let him put aside a chunk of each paycheck so he could build a nest egg that would get him on his feet after graduation. Says Ben: "I liked living at home and it saved me money." Now he puts away part of the $200 or so he earns every two weeks from his job at the campus radio station in hopes of having $7,000 or so saved by graduation. Other students may decide to live in a sorority or fraternity house, where they will constantly be surrounded by some of their closest friends.

- **What's the most convenient place for me to live?**
  Ask yourself where you'll be closest to classes, friends, food, work, and the library. Don't underplay the value of convenience. If you move into a great apartment that's a half-hour's walk from classes, it can be hard to get yourself to lectures on time—or at all.

- **Do I want to be tied to a meal plan?** If you live on campus, you'll probably be required to sign up for some kind of meal plan. Check out the choices that are available to you and, before you sign up for three meals a day, try to be realistic about how often you'll be visiting the dining halls. You don't want to pay for meals you'll never eat. And if you're thinking of skipping the meal plan altogether, ask yourself if you will you ever get a decent meal if you're the one responsible for making it.

- **What services will I give up if I live off campus?** Is there a laundromat available near your apartment, for example? Can you easily and safely get to the library (and home) at night?

- **How will I get to class?** Do you prefer to walk to class or take your bike? You may want to be in a residence hall close to where most classes are held. If you're planning to live off campus, don't forget to factor in any additional transportation costs you'll rack up by commuting.

- **Am I prepared to deal with the responsibilities of having my own place?** Once you're out of the dorms, you'll have to set up your phone and utility services, as well as pay all the bills that come with having an apartment.

Going Solo?

No matter where you live—on campus or off—you have to decide whether or not to have a roommate. Ask yourself:

- **Do I have someone compatible I can live with?** Sharing living quarters can be trying. You want a roommate who has somewhat similar ideas when it comes to things like cleaning, music, overnight guests, and parties. For more ideas on balancing your academic life with your social life and choosing a roommate, check out the Princeton Review's *College Companion*, which deals with topics like drinking and safe sex.

- **Do I want to live alone?** You have to decide if you're tired of sharing living quarters or if you love having a roommate to come home to— someone you can share meals with and talk to about your day. And let's not undervalue having another person around to help if your computer crashes the night before a big paper is due.

- **Can I afford to live alone?** Whether you're talking about a residence hall or a private apartment, it's almost always cheaper to share living quarters with one or more people. Universities generally have single rooms you can try to get into. At the University of Washington, for example, students can choose among doubles, singles, and super singles—essentially nicer, bigger digs that are available for more money—so even on-campus housing offers an option for those who wish to live alone.

How to Find a Place

If you're just going into your freshman year, you'll deal with housing choices by mail with your school. If you're going into your sophomore year or later, you'll have to wade your way through your school's housing allocation system. Check with older students to pick up tips on how to best maneuver through the system. And if you're going to be abroad for any part of the year when housing decisions are made, check with the school about having a friend be your proxy.

To start your housing search:

- **Figure out how much you can afford to spend.** The rule of thumb is that you should spend no more than 30 percent of your income on housing costs. Of course, since you're a student, you probably don't have much of an income. Use the general rule and any budget you've worked up for yourself to figure out how much you can reasonably afford. Rents range all over the place depending on where you live. I know people in

New York City who pay about $1,700 a month for a one-bedroom apartment, while a friend in Minneapolis pays closer to $600 for equivalent space. In smaller towns, you may pay closer to $200 a month. On campus or off, you'll pay based on location and other factors. During the 1997-98 academic year at the University of Arizona, for example, on-campus prices ranged from $2,053 for certain doubles to $4,105 for the nicest singles.

- **Call or stop by your school's housing office and ask whether it helps students find off-campus rentals.** At the University of California at Santa Cruz, registered students can stop by the community rentals office to check listings. The school also counsels students on signing leases and dealing with landlords.

- **Check out any central posting boards on your campus.** At the University of Washington, for example, there's a spot in the Hub—the school's student union—where people list information about apartments.

- **Post your own notice if you're searching for an apartment or roommate.**

- **Check out ads in your campus newspapers, as well as other local papers and publications.** This way you'll get a sense of what kinds of apartments and price ranges are available.

- **Ask friends whose apartments you like if they'll be renewing their lease.** If not, call their landlord or ask them to call for you. If you find an apartment this way, you can avoid the hassle of searching high and low.

- **Do an Internet search for rentals in your town.**

Start Looking Early

This way you'll get a sense of the local housing market and have a range of apartments from which to choose. If you wait too long to look for a place, you may feel rushed into signing a lease for one of the first apartments you see. Or you may get stuck paying more than you've budgeted. If you're staying on campus, you may be able to get a better room by starting early, or at least making sure all your forms are in on time.

Depending on where you live, you may have to pay a broker—an agent who helps you find a place to live. A broker may charge you a percentage of your first year's rent or the equivalent of a month or two of rent. Needless to say, if you can find an apartment without a broker, you can save a pile of money. Keep in mind, however, that a broker can sometimes help you get a good deal that you otherwise wouldn't find on your own.

If you want to stay in your apartment another year, don't forget to renew the lease. Sounds ridiculous? It isn't. Steven Lenard, a student at the University of Chicago, says that one year he and his friends weren't notified that they needed to renew their lease. It wasn't until someone said, "I signed a lease on your apartment," that he realized he and his roommates had lost their place and had to move.

Signing a Lease

A lease (your school may call it something like a residence hall agreement) is a legal contract that covers the most important aspects of living in a rental unit (both on and off campus). It states a number of conditions, including the amount of the rent, whether you can keep pets in the apartment, and how long you are entitled to stay in the property. Leases are pretty intimidating. They are usually printed in small letters and crammed onto only one or a few pieces of paper. And they are usually written in legalese.

While it's not quite as fun as reading your favorite magazine, you do need to read the lease. Yes, before you sign it. Being aware of what it spells out is the only way to guarantee you know exactly what you're getting into. (Some points may apply only to off-campus apartments.)

- **How long is the lease?** Inn-Town Homes, a rental company in Columbus, Ohio, requires students to sign a 12-month lease (and pay their rent over a 10-month period because it's often hard to track down students in the summer).

- **Security deposit.** Many places require you to make a payment that can be equivalent to one or two months' rent as a guarantee you won't trash the apartment. If you move out and leave behind damage, you can kiss all or, at least part, of the money goodbye.

- **Are you allowed to sublet your apartment?** Inn-Town Homes, for example, allows students to sublet, or lease their apartment to another tenant. But some landlords may not let you. Subletting your apartment during the summer when you're away from campus is a good way to recoup some money for the months you have to pay rent but won't be using your apartment.

- **Do you need someone to guarantee the rent?** Some rental companies, especially ones that regularly deal with students, require each roommate to have a responsible adult who guarantees the rent payments will get made.

- **Who is responsible for the maintenance?** Your lease should spell out some of this. Will the apartment be painted before you move in? Who takes care of repairs if the plumbing breaks, for example?

- **What late charges can your landlord impose if you miss your rent due date?** You want to be aware of any and all fees you may be charged.

- **What does the landlord require you to do before you move out?** If you don't follow the requirements, as I wrote above, you may loose all or part of your security deposit. If any of your money is unjustly withheld, however, don't just walk away. When my housemates and I moved out of our junior-year apartment, the landlord refused to return our security deposit. We had left the house in very good condition and refused to believe she found cause to keep our money. She wouldn't budge—until we had an attorney send her a letter on our behalf. Soon after, our check arrived in the mail.

- **If you have roommates, make sure you and each roommate signs the lease.** You don't want to be held responsible for the entire amount of rent if one or more people move out unexpectedly.

Paying Rent

Suffice it to say that it is critical to pay your rent on time. If you don't, you could find yourself being evicted from your apartment—which, as you know, means being kicked out of your home. If you have trouble paying your rent, say there's a problem with your student loan or your parents forget to transfer money to your bank account, call your landlord. Let him know what the problem is and how quickly you can get your payment made. With any luck, you'll find a decent human being on the other end of the line who will cut you a break. Chances are, if you are responsible and honest with your landlord, he or she will be responsive to you.

Setting up Your Apartment or Dorm Room

If you can get yourself together enough to be this organized, before you move in, start thinking about what services you need to have your apartment up and running. About a month before you move, call the local telephone company, utility company, and, if you need it, cable provider to line up an appointment to have your service turned on. Otherwise, you'll be left waiting behind a long line of other students who are moving in and requesting service at the same time. At Ohio State University, for example, tens of thousands of students move into their dorms and apartments around the same time. And, like you, they're all scrambling to get their phone and lights turned on. Someone's going to end up at the back of the line.

Phone Service

If your apartment doesn't yet have phone service, be prepared to pay for the connection. You generally have only one choice for your local phone provider, but you can choose which company you want to handle your long distance calls. An increasing number of areas are opening up to competition for toll or regional calls, phone calls that are too close to be considered long distance and too far away to be considered local.

If you live on campus, your phone service may be up, running, and waiting for you when you arrive. And unlike in a private home, you may not be able to choose your long distance carrier. At the University of Arizona, for example, students like Mike Barnes have AT&T as their carrier. He gets a special code that gives him access to his account from his room (or any friend's room on campus). He just dials in his personal ID code, and the calls he makes get charged directly to him.

The best strategy for cutting your long distance phone bill is to sign up for a discount calling plan. Each of the major carriers—AT&T, MCI, and Sprint—offer special programs that let you earn discounts on the calls you make. But unless you ask for one of the plans you'll probably end up paying full price for your calls. These full-price rates are known as basic or dial 1 rates.

The phone companies are so interested in getting your business (they especially like college students, who tend to call their parents and best friends halfway across the country) that they'll often dangle incentives to get you to switch to their service. Trever Hughes of Duke University says he receives countless mail offers for long distance service and switched from AT&T to another carrier and then back again to AT&T when the company lured him with lower rates. Michael Chant of the University of Wisconsin says he switched to Sprint because the company offered him 200 free minutes. Then AT&T wanted him to switch back—it offered him 120 free minutes a month for six months and a cheaper rate than he was paying. Says Michael: "I jumped back on that bandwagon." Needless to say, special incentives can make it worthwhile for you to switch your phone service.

Follow these tips to make sure you're not paying too much:

- **Call your current long distance carrier and ask if you are signed up for the best calling plan for when you make most of your calls.** If not, ask the company to switch you over to the cheapest plan for your calling habits, whether it provides discounted international calls or calls made exclusively at night.

- **Consider switching to another carrier if it offers you cheaper rates or great incentives, like a substantial number of free minutes.**

- **Make most of your calls at night and on weekends when rates are lower.**

- **When you get an offer for a service that promises to cut your bill if you dial 10 plus a multi-digit code, look carefully at the fine print.** The promised savings are usually compared to the price you would be charged for basic rates from the largest carriers, not the cheaper rates you get if you're signed up for a discount calling plan. And some of these companies have extra fees, like a monthly service charge.

- **If you use a calling card at a pay phone, make sure the long distance carrier listed on the front of the phone is the same as the company that issues your calling card.** If it's not, dial the 800 number listed on the back of your card to connect to your carrier's network. Otherwise, you could end up paying astronomically high rates. And remember, when you use a calling card you're usually hit with a surcharge for the call. Plus, you may pay high per-minute rates.

- **If you make a lot of short calls from a pay phone, consider using a prepaid phone card—debit cards issued by phone carriers for a specified dollar amount and a specified number of calling minutes.** Stick with prepaid cards issued by companies whose names you recognize.

- **Make sure the company whose name appears on your bill is the same one you've signed up to use.** Some companies illegally switch your long distance service without your authorization, a practice known as slamming. If you're slammed, call your local phone company to be switched back to your chosen carrier. Call the company that has slammed you and say you will pay only the rate you would have been charged with your designated carrier.

Furnishing Your Home

When I spoke with Daniel Schmidt, a sophomore at Colby College in Maine, he and his roommate were headed to a used furniture store to look for a couch. "And we're going to scope out the garage sales this weekend." Definitely the right idea. Before you even head to a store, however, check out your parents' basement, your aunt's house, and whatever other attics are accessible to you. Across America, there are an awful lot of old dining room chairs and end tables collecting dust. With any luck, some of them are available to you for free.

Remember too that stores like Kmart have some furniture. And IKEA, the huge home furnishings store, has a great variety of low-priced furniture, kitchen supplies, and all the other things you didn't realize your home needed. If you're on a tight budget, you can find some good buys. But be careful not to buy stuff you don't really need.

Building a Home Theater: Stereo, VCR, TV

College dorm rooms often have a bigger selection of equipment than some small electronics stores—and certainly more than many technologically challenged countries. A few tips to keep in mind:

- **Coordinate with your roommate so you don't both show up with the same equipment.** It's no use having one VCR, let alone two, if you don't have a TV to hook it up to.

- **When shopping for a VCR, focus on picture quality.** There's a big range in the picture quality these machines offer, and you want one that's going to give you the clearest view of rental tapes and shows that you tape off the air.

- **The more features you want, whether in a CD player or a VCR, the more you should expect to spend.** Don't pay extra for fancy features you'll probably never use.

- **For the best prices, shop around and look at some of the big discount stores.** Also check out mass merchandisers like WalMart and Kmart, the warehouse stores like Sam's Club, and catalog outfits. National electronics stores, like Circuit City and Best Buy, often have low prices. Also check out regional chains like Lechmere and Good Guys.

The Budding Gourmet

Mom's kitchen it isn't. Whether you live in a residence hall, where you'll probably want a popcorn machine to help get you through the midnight munchies, or an apartment, where you'll need pots and pans to boil up some spaghetti and pasta sauce, you'll need at least a few items to outfit your space.

Consider what cooking essentials you'll need for your place. Most likely, you don't need china like mom and dad have. If you have roommates, coordinate who will be responsible for bringing, buying, and paying for certain items. You don't necessarily need a microwave, but if you want tea or coffee, you'll need a kettle or a coffee maker. Ask yourself what other items are necessary. And remember, unless you're a gourmet, college isn't the time to stock up on professional quality pots and pans. A few pots, plates, glasses, silverware, and some knives for cutting should serve you well. And don't forget a can opener and a corkscrew.

Protecting Your Stuff (Renter's Insurance)

I was having dinner with a friend recently when the subject of renter's insurance came up. Julia, a recent law school graduate, said she didn't have any insurance. "I don't have anything valuable," she said. Ah, that life were that simple.

Add up all the things you have that aren't valuable, like underwear and books, and you'll realize that the cost of replacing even the small things you keep in your apartment can be pretty hefty. Add in the expensive items like a computer, stereo, television, and VCR and you'll see that you probably own more stuff than you realized. Renter's insurance pays to replace the contents of your apartment if you lose them in a fire, burglary, or other disaster. It also protects you if someone hurts himself in your home and sues you. Despite its very real and practical application, only 41 percent of people who rent apartments have renter's insurance. Help boost the statistic. (Before you buy a policy, however, have your parents check to see if your stuff is covered under their homeowner's insurance policy, as it may be if you live on campus.)

I can hear it now. You're saying you'll chance it. But ask yourself whether the risk is really worth it. Renter's insurance doesn't cost very much when you consider how much you'd pay to replace everything you own if you had a fire or were broken into. Policies can cost less than $150 year, depending on the replacement value of your stuff. And the insurance can really pay off. My friend Anna's apartment near the University of Chicago was broken into last year. The burglar stole her computer, laser printer, VCR, portable CD player, and micro cassette recorder. The day after the break-in, she called her insurance company, which on the spot said it would replace everything. The company bought her a new printer (which was nicer than the one that was stolen), VCR, and portable CD player. Plus, the company gave her a check for $1,200 to cover the value of the computer that was stolen. She pays $120 a year for the policy, which she calls "obviously one of the best investments I ever made."

A renter's insurance policy should also cover items that get stolen when you're away from home, like a bicycle that gets taken downtown or a nice watch that's stolen if you're mugged. Check your policy since there may be limitations on coverage.

You can look in the yellow pages of your phone book to find names of insurance companies. Call a few and ask about the cost and scope of coverage. Also, ask about what discounts you can get if you have a smoke detector and fire extinguisher.

Stop, Thief!

My friend Jerry and I had just moved into the apartment where we were going to spend our senior year. We didn't yet have a routine, so when I came home one night and Jerry didn't say hello when I walked in the apartment, I figured he didn't hear me, was sleeping, or just didn't want to talk. Strange, I thought I'd heard a noise from his room. Turns out, someone had broken into our apartment and was climbing out the window of Jerry's bedroom as I walked in. Only I didn't figure that out until Jerry walked into the apartment from his evening out. It goes without saying that I was extremely lucky that I didn't walk in on whomever was hanging out in Jerry's room and that he (or she) left quickly. Jerry and I were also lucky that our visitor didn't have time to steal anything.

To keep yourself, your apartment, and your belongings safe, be sure to keep the windows and doors locked. If your apartment has an alarm system, use it. And, as your parents probably reminded you a zillion times when you were a kid, don't open the door to strangers.

Fire Drill

Make sure you have a working smoke detector. Ideally, you should check it once a month to see that it works and, once a year, change the batteries. If you have a fire, leave your apartment or dorm room immediately and call the fire department from outside.

A few tips to help prevent fires:

- Don't overload electrical sockets.
- Don't use light bulbs that have a higher wattage than the manufacturers recommend.
- Leave space around your television, computer, stereo, etc.
- Don't leave a fire (in the fireplace or on the stove) unattended.
- Keep a fire extinguisher nearby.
- Be extra careful when you have a barbecue.

Fair Housing—Know Your Rights

The Federal Fair Housing Act says you can't be discriminated against in the sale or rental of housing based on race, color, national origin, religion, sex, family status (meaning people who have children, are pregnant, etc.), or physical disabilities. The law applies to most housing.

Based on these factors, no one can:

- Refuse to rent or sell you housing.
- Refuse to negotiate with you for housing.
- Make a house or apartment unavailable.
- Deny you the house or apartment.
- Set different terms, conditions, or privileges.
- Falsely say the dwelling can't be inspected, sold, or rented.

Buildings with elevators and more than four units and where the first occupants moved in after March 13, 1991 are required to be accessible to people with disabilities. Individuals with disabilities are allowed to make changes to their home or common areas, at their own expense, if the changes are necessary to allow them to use the housing. In some cases, the landlord may require tenants to restore the property to its original condition when they move out.

Alternatives to Renting

If renting an apartment or a house seems like too much of a burden, then you definitely don't want to consider buying a home. I'll mention this topic briefly since most students won't have the option.

Some parents—or a rare student—may choose to buy a home near campus. In the case of buying, you get all the tax benefits of owning a home, like being able to deduct real estate taxes and mortgage interest payments from your taxable income. Instead of paying rent, you use monthly payments to pay off the mortgage and build equity in the house. You can rent out rooms to other students to help defray costs. And, if you're lucky, you can sell the house for a profit.

When he was a sophomore at the State University of New York at Albany, Gary Schatsky bought a six-bedroom house near campus. "Rental prices were relatively high and property prices were relatively low," he says. So he bought a run-down house, got a government-sponsored loan for improvements, fixed it up, and rented out five of the six bedrooms. Says Gary: "I ended up making a nice amount of money." Not only did he make enough from rent payments to cover his tuition, but when he was ready to move Schatsky sold the house for a profit.

Needless to say, buying a house is a big financial commitment. Besides handling the mortgage and taxes, you have to have money set aside to cover insurance, repairs, and maintenance. You should consider buying a house only if you have the financial resources—and the time—to make it a successful venture.

Home Sweet Home

It will take some legwork to get yourself set up in an on-campus residence hall or off-campus apartment, but all the effort will be worth it when you can come home after a grueling day of classes or exams, kick off your shoes, and relax in your own space.

Chapter 7

Smart Shopping

Are you the type of person who shops for sport? A bargain hunter? Someone who enters a store only when your mother threatens to burn your favorite jeans unless you get a new pair without holes? As a college student, you'll be making a lot of purchases. You're probably living away from home for the first time and will need a lot of new things—from sheets and towels to a computer and telephone service. Or if you live at home while going to school, you're probably buying a lot more of your own supplies, like text books and car insurance—even laundry detergent. Shopping isn't just about the stuff that you buy in a store and take home with you. It's also about services, like getting a cable provider and, if you're inclined, a health club membership.

The reality is that shopping is all in your attitude. I'm a really good shopper. The main reason is: I'm not a push-over. I look for good deals. If someone's trying to rip me off, I get angry. I'm willing to negotiate to get what I want. Is this true 100 percent of the time? No. I'll splurge like anyone else. But I keep my impulse shopping under control. What follows are tips to help you do the same.

This chapter is not exhaustive (and some shopping strategies are included in other chapters), but it will give you pointers to ensure that you don't get ripped off for any of the common products and services you're likely to need. And it will get you in the habit of being a more savvy consumer, one who makes smart shopping decisions instinctively.

General Strategies

Okay, so it takes more work than you'd like to be a smart consumer. But if you want to get the best deal possible, save money, and be in control, you'll take a little time now to learn how to put yourself in the driver's seat. Start with a few basics: Always think about what you're buying. Ask yourself whether you need it. Look at the quality. Ever bought a shirt where the seams were barely held together with thread? Consider the price and whether you think the purchase is worth the money. And consider where you might be able to buy it for less. (Do these strategies sound like those outlined in chapter 4 to avoid credit card overspending? They are.)

Sometimes smart shopping just means putting yourself in the right place. I go to the discount stores. I don't care that they aren't the ritziest places in town. I want more for my hard-earned money. I know that if I go to a major department store, I'm going to pay more. I'll do that sometimes if there's a special occasion, like a job interview, and I need a special outfit. Then again, my friend Celeste, prefers the convenience of big stores. It's up to you. But don't let yourself spend more than you really want to or need to. That's what it's all about.

One of the biggest lessons about shopping is that you pay for convenience. Have you compared any of the prices of some of your favorite things in the campus store to the price you'd pay five miles away from campus? Shopping in the campus store is sometimes like being in an airport and realizing you forgot to pack your toothbrush. You're basically a captive audience and can be forced to pay big bucks for a simple purchase like a toothbrush. I was in Ithaca last summer with some friends when one of them got sick. I had to be on campus at Cornell that morning and went to the campus store, where I paid several bucks to get her a small bottle of stomach medicine. Off campus, I'm sure I could have found a much bigger bottle of the same medicine for a lot less money.

So finding the best selection and prices, no matter what you're buying, often means going out of your way to save money. Just where should you look? An excellent question, which brings me to my next topic...

Super Stores

These days, a lot of discounts are being offered by the biggest stores, including those enormous stores that focus on one particular area—like Home Depot for everything related to your house, Barnes & Noble for books, and Staples for office supplies. Plus, there are stores like WalMart and Kmart that have big selections and some cheap prices. And there are warehouse stores, like Costco and Sam's Club, where you pay an annual membership fee for unlimited access to bulk and discounted products that range from food, clothes, and electronics to books, computers, and jewelry.

At the end of the day, the savings from these stores can be substantial. I spoke with one student who rented a car with a few friends at the beginning of a fall semester so they could drive to some nearby discount stores, including Home Depot and Kmart, to stock up on furnishings and other things they needed to decorate their suite. They figured their savings would more than pay for the cost of the rental.

The Art of the Deal

While many of us think negotiating the price of something we want to buy is limited to flea markets, there's lots of room to bargain in stores. I recently went to a major store to buy a watch. As I considered which one I preferred and how much I wanted to spend (since there was a pretty big price difference between the two), the saleswoman asked me to wait. She walked away with the more expensive watch and came back five minutes later with an offer to take 10 percent off the ticketed price. And I hadn't even asked for a discount!

As you'll see in the section below on cars, it's sometimes expected that you won't pay the initial price that's asked. While I'm not telling you to ask a sales clerk at a major department store to give you a discount on a shirt, I am suggesting that there is often room to negotiate. Is one of the buttons on a blouse loose? Point it out to a sales clerk, and she may take off a few dollars.

Never underestimate the importance of complaining. Once when I was buying a couch, I had a slew of headaches. The store first delivered the wrong couch, then it kept telling me incorrect delivery times, and on and on. When I finally had the right couch in my apartment, I marched into the store where I had bought it and asked to speak with the manager. I walked him through the entire story, making him listen to all the hassles I had been through and expressing my frustration that no one had even apologized to me for the inconvenience. In the end, he gave me store credit that was equal to something like 10 or 20 percent of the cost of the couch.

Automobiles

Having a car is an expensive proposition. From car payments to gas to repairs to insurance it seems that as soon as you've finished paying off one bill for your car, you have another. Some weeks it seems like I fork over half my paycheck to my auto mechanic. For some students who commute to campus, a car can be a necessity. For those who live on campus, a car may be a luxury they could live without.

Buying a car is a major purchase that requires you to do your homework. If you're in the market for a car, either new or used, set a budget for yourself. Figure out what you really need. Ask yourself, for example, whether you need a car that will get you back and forth to classes for your remaining years in school or if you are looking to make an investment in a car that can last until your 30th birthday.

Whatever you decide, consider buying a used car. New cars lose a good chunk of their value as soon as they are driven out of the showroom. This is known as depreciation. Because of depreciation you can often get a good deal on a used car. Also, there are now superstores that sell used cars, like CarMax Auto Superstores and AutoNation USA. The downside of buying a used car is that you'll have a smaller selection from which to choose, you may buy a car that has a limited warranty or no warranty at all, and you may buy someone else's problems. If you go the used car route, be sure to have a mechanic you trust examine the condition of the car before you commit to buying it.

If you're buying, check out *Consumer Reports'* annual April auto issue. It gives a review of the current models on the market, warns you against problem used cars, and gives you tips on buying and leasing.

Some general tips to follow when shopping for a new car:

- **Go to more than one dealer and compare prices.** This will help you get a sense of what cars are available and the range of prices.

- **Wait until the end of the model year.** Then you can find dealers offering bargains on their current inventory so they can move old cars off their lots. You'll get a much better deal on a car that's been sitting on the lot compared to one that's just rolled off the assembly line.

- **Choose only the options you really need and want.** Additional features add to the price. Sure it would be nice to have a sun roof and a CD player, but if you're footing the bill, these are probably extras you can live without.

- **Once you get close to choosing a car, bargain from the invoice price up.** If you bargain from the sticker price down, you'll end up paying more than is necessary. Car dealers expect you to do some bargaining. If you don't, you'll end up paying way more than is necessary.

- **If you have an old car, don't discuss trading it in until you've settled on a price for the new car.** This will help you get the best price possible on your new car.

- **Comparison shop for financing.** If you or your parents belong to a credit union, check out what interest rate it is charging for loans. Call a few banks. And speak to the dealer's finance department. Then apply for the loan with the lowest rate and best terms.

Insuring Your Car

If you think owning a car is expensive, wait until you see your insurance bill. Depending upon the range of coverage you have, auto insurance pays to repair your car when it's damaged, covers medical bills for you and other people involved in an accident, and replaces your car if it's stolen or totaled in an accident.

Before you settle on a policy, shop around. *Consumer Reports* (800-807-8050) has an insurance price service. For $12, it gives you a list of insurance companies and those companies' rates to insure you, taking into account such details as your driving record, car make and model, and your age.

Ask any insurance company you talk to about discounts. You may get a price break if you get your insurance policy from the same company that provides your renter's insurance. You may also be able to get a price break for good grades. Michael Chant at the University of Wisconsin, for example, gets a discount on his auto insurance because he maintains a high GPA. Michael says he asked his insurance company if there was a discount for students. When he didn't get the information he wanted, he asked a second time and found out about the deal. He now pays $459 for six months of coverage, about $50 less than the original price he was quoted.

Hit the Road, Jack

But not without your AAA membership. I don't know about your auto mechanic skills, but mine are lacking. So each year I'm careful to renew my auto club membership, which gives me free roadside assistance if I get a flat, for example, and towing when necessary. One winter in college when I had my grandmother's old car, I used my AAA membership three times to get a free tow to the mechanic. Plus, members get maps for trips, no-fee traveler's checks, and other travel assistance with their annual benefits.

One more car tip: When you're filling up the tank don't be lazy. Pump your own gas when possible. It's always cheaper to gas up at a self-service pump.

Buying a Computer

Computers are indispensable for a student. How else can you pound out a quick paper, check out movie reviews online, and send e-mail to your friend who goes to school a thousand miles away? Schools have computer centers on campus, where you often have to fight the noise and the urge to socialize in order to get your work done. So you might want to consider buying your own computer. For many students, life without their own computer can be pretty trying.

You may be able to find good education discounts for computers sold on campus. But don't stop your search at your school's offerings. Ethan Collings, a Pepperdine University student who works in his school's computer store, tells potential buyers: "We've got good prices, but do go out there and check." That's because even with the education discounts that are available, you can sometimes find cheaper computers at computer superstores that specialize in bulk computer sales, like CompUSA, and from manufacturers like Dell and Gateway that sell their machines directly to consumers by phone and online.

Most people don't need the fanciest computers with all the latest bells and whistles. Before finalizing your computer deal, ask yourself:

- **What operating system do I want?** You'll have to choose between Macintosh and Windows. Be sure you pick the system that you like and that is compatible with what's generally available on your campus in terms of software and technical support.

- **How much memory and speed do I need?** To meet your basic needs and then some, you probably don't need the fastest computer on the market. Consider one of the low-end computers growing in popularity, machines that sell for under $1,000 because they don't have the fastest chip or modem. Compaq and Packard Bell NEC models were dominating the market at the time of this writing.

- **How much extra can I afford to pay for the latest technology?** It's fun to have the fastest computer on your floor, but remember that you'll be paying for technology that will soon be outdated.

- **Do I need a laptop?** If you're going to be taking notes on your computer during class or writing papers in the library, focus your search on a laptop.

- **Do I need a printer or can I use one in a campus computer lab?** If you buy a printer, you'll need to choose between an ink jet printer, which prints in color, and a laser printer, which has better resolution and prints more quickly. You can also consider a combination machine that incorporates printing, scanning, and faxing capabilities.

- **Do I like the return policy of the store and/ or manufacturer from whom I bought the computer?** You want to know that you have some recourse if your computer gives you problems soon after you get it home. Ask your friends about the experiences they've had. And check out some of the many magazines that carry extensive computer coverage.

Software

Don't be misled by the value of software that's bundled in a computer package. First of all, you may be getting a scaled-down version of the programs that are included. Plus, you probably won't be using a lot of them.

As a student, you'll qualify for some great education discounts for software. When I spoke with Ethan Collings at Pepperdine, for example, he said students at his school could buy Microsoft Office for $199. He put the suggested retail price closer to $500. Check out the offerings on your campus.

School Supplies

In the blink of an eye, you can spend hundreds of dollars on textbooks. But before you run to the campus store and buy every book that's on the syllabus of every class you're taking, wait until you hear from your professors which books you'll really need. If you're only going to read one chapter from a book, you can read that assignment in the library. The same goes for other textbooks you don't want to own. Shop around for used textbooks. Look in off-campus stores nearby that may carry the books you need at a discount.

Besides books, you'll end up spending a lot of money on computer paper, notebooks, pens, and all the other office supplies that, on their own, don't seem so expensive until you find yourself at the cash register facing a bill for well over $100. If you can get to one of the discount stores, like Staples, stock up on all the pens and paper clips you plan to use and you'll save a pile of money.

Beauty Supplies

Beauty comes at a price. Sure, soap is cheap. But some bottles of shampoo can set you back the equivalent of three hours' wages. Try to stock up on all the personal care items you need when you're at a discount store. These places usually have a good selection. Also, look for stores' generic versions of some products, like shampoos and moisturizers.

Food for Thought

Whether you're cooking for yourself all the time or just stocking the fridge for midnight snacks, the best way to cut your food bills is to stay away from prepared foods and fancy products. Basic pasta and canned tomatoes are a lot cheaper than buying fancy, fresh pasta and imported cheese from the nearby gourmet store. And eating in is usually cheaper than eating out.

Josh Kinsler of the University of Virginia realized that when it came to getting his meals it was cheaper to stay close to home (or at least the stove). "Food definitely isn't cheap, so it's hard," he says. "I try to limit fast food and ordering in. It saves me a lot of money if I don't do that." What's on the menu? A lot of tuna salad and hamburgers. It can also be healthier to eat food cooked at home, especially if the alternative is a hamburger, french fries, and a milkshake from your favorite greasy spoon.

When Clothes Make the Man

Sure the *GQ* advertisements look enticing. And there's more personal attention at some of the ritziest stores. But if you're on a tight budget, there are plenty of places to find clothing bargains. Discount stores abound. Then there's the proliferation of discount outlet malls that offer you dozens of stores, some enticing price breaks, and newer styles than you may find at flea markets and second-hand stores.

One of the best ways to save money on clothing is to avoid buying the season's latest styles. Stores put out their fall clothes before summer's over, and they carry their full price tag before the season starts. As the season gets going, the clothes go on sale. That's your chance to go bargain hunting.

Entertainment

You can't really find a cheaper concert ticket. But you can do a few things to cut down on the cost of entertainment. See if you can buy tickets at the box office instead of paying a service charge to get tickets by phone. Scope out any second-run or discount movie theaters near campus. That will shave a few dollars off the cost of a movie ticket. Ask if there are student discounts, as there sometimes are at theaters or museums. Cut out coupons for restaurants that run in local newspapers and magazines. And see if you can work as an usher at a local theater—you may be able to see concerts and plays for free on top of earning some extra cash.

Joining a Health Club

There's a good chance your campus has athletic facilities you can use. And they're probably far cheaper than joining a private gym. But if you're thinking of joining a health club, here are a few tips to keep in mind:

- **Look for a club that is close to home or school.** If it's not convenient, chances are you won't use the facilities after your initial enthusiasm wears off.

- **Take a tour of the club and be sure to check it out during the hours you're likely to use it.**

- **Don't feel pressured to join the first time you look at a facility.** Health clubs often push "specials" that are about to expire. But chances are, when you're ready to join, there will be some kind of price break going on at that time. Don't let a pushy salesman force you into signing a contract.

- **Speaking of contracts, read it carefully before you sign**.

- **Work out safely.** Drink lots of water. If you have an injury, rest.

The Payoff

Consider shopping a sport in which your goal is to spend the least for the best return. You win if your jeans last as long as you need them to, if you don't overspend on your food budget, and you save enough money to buy that new CD you've been wanting. Spending money is not bad. As a matter of fact, it's quite fun. But it's even more fun when you get a great deal.

Chapter 8

Consumer Protection

You may not bring home a regular paycheck, but that's not going to stop individuals and companies from trying to take advantage of you and whatever money you do have. This chapter is intended to help you avoid getting ripped off. It will spell out some of the laws that are in place to protect you as a consumer and give you tips to separate legitimate sales pitches from scam operations.

Cutting through the hype

Whether by phone, mail, or advertisement, the pitches come fast and furiously. "Stuff envelopes at home and make a fortune." "You've already won!" And the list goes on and on.

Deciphering marketing pitches requires the use of common sense. Say you get what looks like a check in the mail for a large amount of money. Chances are slim to none that someone you know actually sent you the check without your knowledge. And there's about a zero chance some random company wants you to have, say, $25,000. So if you look more closely, you'll see the check is just part of some marketing hype intended to lure you into whatever sales literature hides behind the enticing (and fake) check.

Companies that run sweepstakes, for example, use any number of tricks to entice you to their wares. Some common ploys: Bogus checks, envelopes that look like they were sent by some private express service, urgent messages that make you think you've already won a prize, and packages that appear to be sent from a government agency.

Bottom line: Whether you're reading a newspaper advertisement, listening to a sales pitch on the telephone, or opening a piece of mail, it pays to be skeptical. Here are basic rules to keep you out of trouble:

- If any deal sounds too good to be true, it is.

- Never give your bank account number to any salesperson.

- Don't give out your credit card information unless you've initiated the transaction (like when you walk into a store or call a mail-order company to make a purchase). If, however, you decide to make a purchase you did not initiate, a credit card will give you some protection if you later have a dispute with the marketer.

- Never send cash or let someone come to your home to pick up a payment.

- Always read advertisements with a critical eye.

- Always read the fine print of any mail offers that interest you. It should spell out all of the important information you need. In a sweepstakes, for example, it should state whether or not the prize is guaranteed. If critical information is missing, throw the offer away.

- Be extra careful about travel offers that are pitched to you and sound like they are free or being sold for bargain-basement prices. The National Fraud Information Center suggests that if you never heard of the company offering a trip, don't sign up.

- If you've already been victimized by a company, be especially careful of any subsequent offers pitched to you by that or other companies. People who have fallen prey to scams often end up on "sucker lists" and are targeted by other shady companies, some that have paid big bucks to get their name and phone number or address.

- When in doubt about any offer, walk away. That will give you time to consider whether an offer is legitimate. You can call the Better Business Bureau to see if there is a history of complaints against the company, a local consumer protection agency to check out a company's reputation, or even your state attorney general's office. Phone numbers for government agencies are listed in the blue pages of the phone book.

- When it comes to sweepstakes, you never have to make a purchase to enter.

Buyer Beware

There are a number of ways you can be taken advantage of. A few popular ones:

- 900 numbers. Don't call unless you want to rack up expensive telephone charges.

- Pyramid schemes. Be wary of companies that say you can make a lot of money by selling its products and earn a commission by getting others to sell the goods. Don't pay for any starter kits.

- Credit repair offers. The only offers of help you should accept for repairing your credit are from nonprofit credit counseling services. No one can wipe the slate clean for you, no matter how much you pay.

- Travel offers. Who wouldn't love to win a free trip to the Bahamas? If you call the phone number listed, you may find yourself being encouraged to join an expensive travel club—or worse.

- Foreign lotteries. You can't legitimately enter a foreign lottery, so don't be enticed by any of the growing number of offers promising you a share of the world's richest lottery pots.

- Internet scams. Because the Internet is cheap to use, con artists are now making a home for themselves there. Scams run the gamut, from get-rich-quick schemes to false claims that you've won fabulous prizes.

Legal Protections

There are a host of federal and state laws intended to protect consumers, including deceptive trade statutes in each state and federal postal regulations that prohibit companies from sending mail that looks like it comes from the U.S. government. Still, there are many gaps in the laws that exist.

In an effort to fight fraud in telemarketing, the Federal Trade Commission—the federal agency charged with protecting consumers—has put in place a Telemarketing Sales Rule. The law is intended to shield you from both annoying and deceptive telemarketing practices. According to the Telemarketing Sales Rule:

- It's illegal for a telemarketer to call you if you specifically ask not to be called.

- Telemarketers can call you only between 8 a.m. and 9 p.m. (Sure, as a college student, your day is just beginning at 9 p.m. But for the rest of the world this is cause to say "Hallelujah!")

- Telemarketers are required to tell you that they are making a sales call and who is trying to sell you something.

- They cannot misrepresent any information.

- You must be told the total cost of the products or services being sold, as well as restrictions on getting or using them. In a prize promotion, you must be told the odds of winning or that no purchase is necessary to win.

- Telemarketers may not withdraw money from your checking account without your verifiable authorization.

- They cannot lie to get you to pay.

Remember, if someone calls you and you don't want to be bothered, it's your right to hang up. And you can ask a company to place you on its "Do Not Call" list, which should eliminate annoying sales calls from that particular business.

Stopping the Deluge

You can cut down on the junk calls and mail you get by signing up for a telephone or mail preference service that's offered by the Direct Marketing Association. These take you off major telephone and mailing lists.

To cut down on the number of telemarketing calls you receive, write to:

Telephone Preference Service
P.O. Box 9014
Farmingdale, New York 11735-9014

You can also get off most of the major mailing lists by writing to:

Mail Preference Service
c/o Direct Marketing Association
P.O. Box 9008
Farmingdale, New York 11735-9008

Where to Complain

If you think you've been victimized by a company, call your state attorney general's office to complain. You can also call the National Fraud Information Center at 800-876-7060. Check out the organization's web site at www.fraud.org. This organization helps consumers file complaints with the appropriate government agencies. You can also check your local phone directory to contact the Better Business Bureau. You can also visit their web site at www.bbb.org. Finally, you can write to the Consumer Response Center, Federal Trade Commission, Washington, D.C. 20580.

Chapter 9

Healthy Choices

By one estimate, at least one-third of college students are uninsured or underinsured (meaning they don't have adequate coverage to pay their medical expenses when and if they get sick or injured). Don't be part of that crowd. Even one visit to the doctor can cost you hundreds of dollars and a major illness or injury can wipe out your family's resources. This chapter will help you sort out what health coverage you already have, what you need, what your school provides, and what happens if you get sick and don't have adequate insurance. Health insurance may not be the most exciting topic, but it's truly one of the most important.

What Are My Choices?

Health insurance pays the cost of your medical care. There are generally two kinds of coverage: fee-for-service and managed care. With fee-for-service plans, you can go to the doctor of your choice and, after the visit, submit a claim to have the bill paid by the insurance company. With this type of arrangement, you are responsible for part of the payment—typically 20 percent. And before your insurance company will even start to pay the bills, you first must reach a deductible—the amount of medical expenses you pay out of pocket every year before your insurance kicks in. For example, if you have a $250 deductible, you pay the first $250 of your medical bills, and the insurance company picks up 80 percent of the rest.

There are different types of managed care policies, including health maintenance organizations (HMOs) and preferred provider organizations (PPOs). Both of these plans are structured to encourage you to use doctors affiliated with the plan. When you see doctors on an approved list you make a co-payment that is typically about $10. In an HMO, you generally have a primary care doctor who coordinates your treatment and must approve visits to specialists. In a PPO, you pay less to see doctors who are in the insurance company's network of physicians. You also have the option to go to a doctor outside the approved network, but you'll have to pay a bigger share of the bill.

Do I Already Have Insurance?

Check to see if you have proper health insurance before you find yourself in the doctor's office or emergency room. Preferably, check it out before you leave for college. If you're reading this and have already enrolled in school, it's not too late to ask. The key is to find out before you need to use your policy. "All it takes is a skiing accident or an auto accident or something of that nature and they'll [students] find they don't have the insurance they need," says Cyndy Launchbaugh, communications director for the Chickering Group, a Cambridge-based student health insurance provider. "You should not take for granted that you are adequately covered." Do you want to start asking about your health insurance when you're doubled over in pain with stomach troubles or screaming your lungs out because of a broken leg? Graphic images, but motivational. Ask now.

The first step in getting a handle on your health insurance needs is to figure out what coverage you already have. It can come from:

- Your school's student health center
- A student health insurance policy
- A parent's policy
- A spouse's policy
- Your own coverage from an employer
- Coverage from the military

Have your parents check their health insurance policy to see if you are covered under their plan. Children are often insured under their parents until they are 19. For students, the coverage may extend until age 23. That saves good money for people like Ben Roberts. The University of Alaska student we first mentioned in the housing chapter is covered under his dad's health plan. And because he goes to school in his hometown of Anchorage, he gets to go to the same doctors he's always used.

But coverage under your parents' policy doesn't guarantee that you're adequately protected. Unless it's an emergency, many insurance plans require you to see doctors affiliated with them—an impossibility much of the time if you go to a school that's some distance from your family and your normal coverage area. So if your parents' health insurance policy is a regional plan, say an HMO, non-emergency visits to doctors and related services near your campus may not be covered. Before you leave for school, have your parents find out what doctors you can see both at home and near school for both emergency and non-emergency situations.

If you are married and your spouse has a job with insurance, check to see what kind of coverage it provides for you. If you have a full- or part-time job, ask someone in your benefits office what you have or can get in terms of health insurance and how much it will cost. If you don't have coverage, and you or your parents are part of a religious, professional, or other group, ask if it offers any group health insurance. Group plans are usually cheaper than the cost of buying individual coverage. We'll talk more about how to get additional coverage if you need it later in this chapter.

Student Health Centers

Campus student health centers typically offer primary care, the services you would normally turn to a family doctor for, such as treatment for an earache or a twisted ankle. Small student health facilities may have a nurse, an exam room, and a doctor who visits campus a few hours a week. Larger facilities may offer fairly extensive services, such as full-time doctors and nurses, specialists like allergists and dermatologists who visit campus regularly, birth control counseling, psychological services (though the school may limit the number of visits you can make), a pharmacy, and AIDS testing. Take a little time to see what services your campus health center offers so that when you need care, you'll know where to turn.

Payment for on-campus health services is either included in your tuition or billed as a separate student health fee. Depending on your school, it can range from about $20 a year to several hundred dollars a year. "On average, the fee is around $120," says Brett Prager, chief executive officer of College Health Care, a Connecticut-based company that manages student health centers at several campuses across the U.S.

On top of the base cost, you may have to pay extra for some of the non-basic medical services that are offered on your campus. If you need an X-ray and can have it done in the health center, for example, you may be charged. There's a good chance you'll have to pay for prescription medications. And if you need a throat culture, don't be surprised if you're charged for the test.

No matter how extensive your campus health services are, however, they still don't replace the need for private insurance. Student health services have limited resources. If you need to see a doctor who doesn't visit the center or you need to be admitted to the hospital, for example, you'll need a means of paying for those services.

When You Need More Than Your Health Center Offers

As you just read, student health centers are designed to handle primary care needs. And if you go to school away from home, your parents' plan may not cover you for the non-emergency medical care you need to seek off campus. If this is the case, you should definitely consider getting a separate student health insurance policy, a private insurance plan that covers you for off-campus medical care. Many schools offer them, and some schools even require them.

If you think you can go without, think again. Worst-case scenario: you get hit by a car or catch malaria during some exotic trip. If you end up in the hospital, you're going to rack up thousands of dollars in bills. If you don't have insurance to cover the expenses, even double shifts at Burger King will barely make a dent in those bills.

Like approximately 25 percent of colleges, Montana State University in Bozeman requires its students to have health insurance. If registered students can't show proof of coverage, they must buy the $300-a-semester Blue Cross plan offered by the school. Students who buy the plan for both semesters of the academic year also get coverage in the summer. (Not all plans include coverage for the summer. If yours doesn't, see if you can pay extra to be covered during those months or look into getting a short-term major medical policy, which is described below.)

Hilary Krieger spends about $600 a year to buy the policy offered through Cornell University because it's cheaper than being carried on her parents' plan. "It's definitely helped me," she says. How much? Hilary works crazy hours as editor-in-chief of *The Cornell Daily Sun*. Most likely as a result of sleep deprivation, she had to fight off a bout of mono that forced her to stay overnight at the student health center. Plus, she needs allergy shots on a regular basis. Her insurance policy pays for it all.

At the University of Florida in Gainesville, students who sign up for health insurance have two choices. They can pay $140 a year for a plan that covers the pay-for-service aspects of the on-campus health center, such as laboratory work and visits to specialists. For more complete coverage, they can pay $583 a year for all the pay-for-service features of the health center, plus hospital coverage.

Don't assume that just any old plan will give you all the coverage you need. "These school insurance plans need to be carefully reviewed before they're considered for your sole insurance coverage," says Jim Mitchell, director of the student health service at Montana State and, at the time of this writing, president of the American College Health Association. "If the plan is cheap, you better look carefully." Some plans have low hospital benefits or don't cover sports injuries, for example. And some have low caps on the total amount they'll pay for your care. Ask someone at your campus health center about options for supplemental coverage or have your parents see what additional coverage you are eligible for under their policy.

If You Study Abroad

If you're going overseas for a semester or year, be sure to see if your current policy pays for doctor visits or hospitalization in another country. If not, you'll need to find a policy that covers you while you're away. Ask your school's international studies office if it has information on insurance plans that pay if you get sick overseas or if it has details about getting insurance in the country you'll be visiting. If you need more leads, call the consulate of the country that you'll be traveling to or ask other students who have already traveled there to see what you can find out.

When I was studying overseas at age 24, I was covered under my mother's health insurance plan for the first part of my year away because I was a registered student who was still under 25. When my birthday came, however, her plan kicked me out. I bought a local policy that covered me for the remainder of my time away and, when I returned to the United States, picked up a short-term major medical policy that would pay for big bills, like a hospital stay. You'll read about these plans below.

If You Have No Coverage

Some people think it's acceptable to go without health insurance. It's not. While it's true that you can usually get medical attention in almost any hospital emergency room, you're going to be billed for the visit whether you have insurance or not. And it's not so easy to walk away from the charges. Jim Mitchell of Montana State says he knows of cases where students have lost their cars or computers to hospitals collecting payments from students who didn't pay their bills. You know it's your responsibility to pay the bills you rack up. But did you know that information about unpaid medical bills can end up on your credit report?

Insurance You Can Live Without

If anyone tries to sell you life insurance (a policy that pays cash in the event you die), you can bet they're not looking out for your best interests. The only people who need life insurance are those who have other people dependent on them for income. Say you're a student who has a spouse and kids that rely on your current income or potential future earnings, you may need a policy. And if you're a famous Hollywood actor who produces enough income to support your parents and siblings, you may be worth insuring. But if you're a 20-year-old student with no spouse and no kids (and not even a decent CD collection), there's little reason even to consider life insurance.

Short-Term Policies

Short-term major medical policies are specifically geared to providing coverage during short periods of time when you don't otherwise have health insurance, like the summer or the period after you graduate when you're looking for a job. They are intended to cover major medical expenses, like hospital stays. Short-term policies have limitations. They often limit coverage for preventive care, such as routine physicals. They may not, for example, pay for pregnancy care or dental work. They may have lower lifetime caps on coverage. These plans are intended to get you through short periods when you don't have a comprehensive health insurance plan, but still need protection against a medical catastrophe.

Policies from Golden Rule Insurance, for example, cover you for one- to six-month periods. And if you still don't have coverage when the policy term expires, the company will let you renew once. Before the insurance company starts to pay benefits, you first have to meet a deductible for each illness or injury. The higher the deductible, the lower your payments or premiums for your policy. As of this writing, a 24-year-old woman in Alaska, for example, pays $69.61 a month for a Golden Rule policy with a $250 deductible. The payments drop to $54.74 a month if she has a $500 deductible and $37.11 a month if she has a $1,000 deductible.

Ask your school for suggestions on good short-term or catastrophic insurance policies. Or go online and search for information. You can also ask friends or have your parents ask their insurance company for recommendations.

After You Graduate

When you graduate, you'll probably fall off your parent's policy and lose any benefits you had from a student health insurance plan. Remember Rachel Aydt from the chapter on managing debt? She took the first real job that was offered to her after graduation so she could have health insurance. "I was really nervous," she says of walking around without coverage. And she was lucky she got her policy when she did. Soon after her insurance kicked in, she broke her arm and racked up a bunch of medical bills that were covered by her new policy.

If you don't have a job right away (or a job that gives you immediate health insurance benefits), you'll need to get some kind of gap coverage. You may be able to pay to extend coverage from your parents' plan under COBRA, a federal program that, among other things, requires companies with more than 20 employees to extend coverage of a person who is no longer considered a dependent under the policy and doesn't qualify for another group health insurance plan. Otherwise, you can consider a short-term major medical policy. Check with your school's alumni association, which may offer insurance policies to its members at special rates.

Learn the System

Whatever kind of coverage you have, you'll save yourself a lot of hassle and money if you take a little bit of time to learn a few things about your policy before you start to use it. A few things to consider:

- What is your deductible?

- Are you required to use certain doctors in order for the insurance to pay for treatment?

- Do you have to make a co-payment when you visit a doctor, meaning are you responsible for part of the doctor bill? Plans typically charge about $10 for each visit to a doctor in the health insurance company's network of approved physicians.

- Are there particular hospitals you should use in case of an emergency?

- Which medical services require you to get prior approval before you receive treatment?

- Does your plan pay for preventive care? If you are a woman, for example, will your plan pay for an annual gynecological checkup?

- Does the plan pay for dental work?

- Does it pay for eye exams, eye glasses, or contacts?

- Do you have to have one doctor who is responsible for your primary medical care and who must refer you to specialists for your coverage to kick in?

- How do you get reimbursed if you have to lay out money for an office visit or other treatment?

- What coverage limitations exist if you have a preexisting condition, an illness that has already been diagnosed?

Again, know these things before you need to. I hope the only things you'll end up using your health insurance for are annual doctor visits. But you wouldn't want to find out how much you need coverage by not having it.

Chapter 10

Fun in the Sun

You've worked hard. You've survived Econ 101. Your friends are planning a big getaway to Cancun for spring break. And all you can think about is working on your tan. But, whoa, have you seen the price of those plane tickets? Before you book your trip, take a look at this chapter to find out how to scout out cheap fares, exchange currency, and get all the discounts you can possibly scrounge up.

Student Discounts

When it comes to travel, companies and institutions shower students with price breaks. From special youth fares on airlines to discounted museum admissions, your teens and early 20s are the time to pay less than the rest of the folks. I remember being laughed at by one of my first editors for qualifying for a price break. I was a reporter just out of college and had to go to Washington, D.C. for a conference. I knew the airline I was flying had a special youth fare on its shuttle. I'd taken advantage of it when I was still in school and even after graduation since I was still within the age limit. So I showed proof of my age when buying the ticket for my business trip and paid the cheaper fare. When I handed in my expense report, my editor thought the idea of a professional journalist getting the youth fare was the funniest thing. He'd never known an employee to come even close to qualifying. What can I say? I'm always looking for a bargain, no matter who's footing the bill.

Get Carded—The Good Way

Many times your student ID card is enough to get a discount. You know the drill. You pull out your card at a local pizza store or flash it to get a cheaper admission to the local museum. And, in many places, your school card alone gets you a cheaper price. But don't stop there. Look into getting a Student Advantage card (800-333-2920). For $20, at the time of this writing, you get discounts from 15,000 businesses, including Amtrak, Greyhound, stores, and restaurants throughout the U.S. (As of this writing, AT&T had agreed to a three-year deal in which it would pay the fee for a Student Advantage membership for students who became new long-distance, calling card, or credit card customers.) And for students who have it, the discounts are nothing to sneeze at. Ilana Silver, whom we met in chapter 4, says she regularly uses her card to shave money off the cost of a round-trip train ticket between Delaware, where she goes to school, and New York, where her parents live. The amount she saves on the train trips alone—15 percent—more than pays for the card. So all the discounts she gets for other purchases are like money in her pocket.

To qualify for the most discounts possible when traveling overseas, make sure you have an International Student Identity Card. These cards open up a world of cut rates and travel benefits. You can get the card through Council

Travel (888-268-6245), or STA (800-781-4040), a student-focused travel agency that has offices near many college campuses. You can also check out both companies' web sites for information about Eurail passes and a host of other student-focused travel advice. At the time of this writing, the card cost $20, an amount you can more than earn back with just a few purchases or museum admissions during your trip. Before you say no thanks, remember that sooner or later on your trip to Paris you'll probably find yourself trudging through the Louvre in search of the Mona Lisa. The card also comes with some basic insurance for illness and accidents, and you can buy additional insurance coverage.

The discounts, however, can be region-specific. My friend Bruce says he couldn't find many places that would give him a student discount during a big trip he took to southeast Asia. But for him and the hordes of other students who have traveled through Europe, it pays off handsomely.

If you plan to stay in hostels—where students and travelers can find cheap and collegial lodging throughout the world—don't forget to get an International Youth Hostel Card. It gives you admission to the network of affiliated hostels around the world at the member rate. With your membership, you get a listing of hostels throughout the U.S. and Canada, a toll free number you can use to make reservations at selected hostels, and discounts on a variety of purchases and admission fees. For more information, contact Hostelling International/American Youth Hostels (202-783-6161).

Joy of Flying

You may love it or hate it, but when it comes to getting someplace far away, you can't beat the joys—or at least the speed—of air travel. The problem with taking a plane is the expense. Airline costs vary widely, with the same route potentially costing vastly different amounts on different airlines. Translation: Learn how to work the system so you end up in the cheap seats. The major ways to cut costs:

- **Look for sales.** Airlines routinely cut their fares, and when one airline announces it is lowering prices, the other major airlines often follow right behind. Watch newspaper ads for sales and try to buy your ticket during an airline price war. That way, you can save money over the normal, full-price fares.

- **Buy advance purchase tickets.** If you buy a 21-day or 14-day advance purchase ticket, for example, you'll pay significantly less than if you book a ticket at the last minute. Airlines make a lot of money from business travelers and others who don't know ahead of time when they'll be traveling. Unlike you, these people are willing or sometimes don't have a choice but to pay top dollar to get to their destinations.

- **Stay over a Saturday night.** Call it quirky, but one of the fastest and easiest ways to slash the price of a plane ticket is to extend your stay over a Saturday night. And while you may need to find a place to stay for another night, you should be able to cut your fare enough to more than cover the expense of an extra night's lodging (that is, if you can't find a friend's floor to crash on).

- **Consider flying to a close, but less expensive destination.** Remember Morris Feldman from the first chapter? When he's flying home from the University of Chicago to Fayetteville, Arkansas, Morris finds out the price of flying directly home, as well as the cost of flying into nearby Tulsa, Oklahoma. If it's significantly cheaper, which it usually is, Morris says it's worth the extra time and gas money for his parents to drive two extra hours to pick him up in Tulsa.

- **Sign up for one of the online updates offered by some airlines.** My brother Gary is signed up for the online services offered by American, Continental, and US Airways. Every week, he gets an e-mail message from each airline that tells him about last-minute, weekend travel specials.

He also gets information on deals to use frequent flier miles, say 1,000 points, to qualify for some price break.

- **Ask if there's any way to lower the fare.** Last spring, when I was booking plane tickets to Italy, the fare was a wee bit on the high side. Not wanting to compromise how many cappuccinos I could afford to sip at Italian cafes, I asked the rep for TWA (they were having a great sale) if there was any way to lower the price. She did a few tricks on her computer and said that if I flew back to New York from Rome on a Monday instead of Sunday, I could get a round-trip ticket for just over $500. That was several hundred dollars less than the price I'd originally been quoted for the Sunday return.

Credit Card Vouchers

Student credit card solicitations routinely offer vouchers for discount plane tickets. If you fly, it can definitely make sense to sign up for a card that runs one of these promotions. When he was in business school at New York University, my brother Gary signed up for a student Optima card and got discount travel certificates for Continental. He used the vouchers for separate trips to San Francisco and Tucson—and earned frequent flier miles for the flights. The vouchers do have restrictions, however. They expire. They have blackout dates. And, when he used them, reservations could only be made within 21 days of departure. But, hey, you're living the high life of a student. You don't need to plan your life too far in advance. If you use up your vouchers, call your card company and ask if it will give you more.

Couriers and Consolidators

If you're feeling adventurous, don't have to stick to a particular schedule, and don't need to carry much baggage, check out flying with a courier service. In exchange for a cheap airline ticket, you agree to carry packages and documents to other cities or countries. The service makes all the arrangements and gives you a discounted plane ticket in exchange for your checked baggage space.

The hitch is that you often can't solidify your travel plans until the last minute. And because the courier service will be using your baggage space to transport its packages, you may be limited to taking only carry-on luggage.

My friend Jerry Lazore used a courier ticket to get to Spain. To learn about his options, he bought a book that explained the ins and outs of couriers. Once he settled on a company he wanted to use, Jerry checked out its record with the Better Business Bureau. In the end, he got his ticket for hundreds of dollars less than he would have paid for a regular ticket. Jerry says being a courier works best if you have the freedom to go at a moment's notice. Then you can call a courier company and see which destinations it has available and, within days, leave for some exotic locale.

The other C word in airline lingo is consolidator. These are companies that buy seats in bulk from airlines and sell them to individuals at a discount. Most people use consolidators for international travel. When Eric Lundberg of the University of Wisconsin was going to Paris he found an amazing deal from a consolidator and ended up paying just $435 round trip for a flight from Madison to Paris. You can usually find lists of consolidators in the travel section of the newspaper. Also, check out the phone book and the Internet.

Using a consolidator ticket isn't as flexible as a regular ticket. Newspaper ads from consolidators probably don't say which airline you'd be flying for a particular route, so be sure to ask which carrier has available seats. You may only feel comfortable flying airlines you've heard of. You may not be able to earn frequent flier miles for your trip or order a special meal. Also, ask what protection you'll have if the flight is canceled—the carrier, for example, may not help you get on another flight if you're traveling with a consolidator's ticket as it would if you had purchased your ticket directly from the airline.

If you use a consolidator or a courier, definitely check the company's record with the Better Business Bureau or a local consumer protection office, whose phone number you can find in the blue pages of your local phone book. Also, use a credit card to purchase your ticket. That way, if you have a problem with your ticket or with the company, you'll have your credit card company to help fight your battle.

Frequent Flier Miles

For some people it's a game. For others, it's an obsession. No matter how you approach it, racking up frequent flier miles can help get you get to your destination for free. In the credit card chapter, we talked about earning miles with a credit card linked to an airline program. These days it seems everyone—not just your credit card company—is throwing miles at you. Besides earning miles when you fly or charge on a credit card linked to a frequent flier program, you can also get them for renting cars and using a particular long-distance phone service.

The best way to accrue enough miles to earn a free ticket is to stick to one carrier instead of spreading out the miles over various programs. If you grew up in Texas and go to school in Maine, you'd rack up a lot of miles just going back and forth a few times a year, for example. But never fly on a particular airline just to earn miles. If you can get a cheaper ticket to get to your destination on another carrier, buy it. To help you figure out the math: The rule of thumb is each frequent flier mile is worth 2 cents.

As you'll discover when you first try to use miles for a free seat, they can be hard to cash in for a ticket. It varies by airline, but as of this writing it's common to need 25,000 miles for a free domestic ticket (and many more for an international seat). Airlines have blackout dates when you can't use your miles. And they leave only a limited number of seats available on each flight for people using frequent flier miles. So once you have enough miles to redeem, you have to see if you can even get a reservation. So book early. And be flexible. When I was going to Colorado for Thanksgiving, I had enough miles to cash in for free seats, but couldn't fly back on Sunday night. That's when the rest of the world is willing to pay big bucks to get home in time for work and school on Monday morning. To use the miles, the airline could only find me a seat if I agreed to fly home on Monday.

No matter how much of a hassle it is to redeem miles, go ahead and dream of all the exotic places you may be able to fly for free. Celeste Sollod, my editor, usually uses the miles she accrues to fly from New York to California to visit her family. But she's hanging on to her dream of having enough time and enough miles at some point in the near future to fly to Holland for an extensive bike trip.

Before you redeem miles, do the math. If the ticket you're trying to get for free isn't too expensive, you may want to purchase tickets and save your frequent flier miles for a later, more expensive trip. Check, however, to see when the miles expire.

Travel Services

Finally, don't think you have to make all reservations yourself. Get to know a good travel agent. Travel agents, who usually get a commission that's paid by the companies whose trips you are booked on, have access to all airline seat availability and prices and a host of other trip information. Besides booking your transportation, travel agents also may have great recommendations about where to stay and eat. When my friend Debbie and I were planning a trip to Costa Rica, we found a travel agent who specialized in the country. (Because we didn't know anyone who had used this travel agent, I called the Better Business Bureau to see if he had a record of complaints.) Using a travel agent got us a fun trip that we probably couldn't have put together ourselves. We stayed at a great and affordable lodge near an active volcano, went hiking in the cloud forest, and took a boat ride through the jungle on our way to a remote nature preserve.

Now there are also online travel agencies where you can get information on hotels, bed and breakfasts, air travel, and car rentals. You can search for ideas, look for discounts, and make reservations.

Getting Home: Buses and Trains

Sometimes you can't wait to get home to mom's cooking and your childhood bed. The question is, how to get there without going broke or blowing a whole day traveling. Brown University student Elana Rosenfeld Berkowitz chooses between the bus and the train to get from Providence to her parents' apartment in New York City. Not surprisingly, the bus is cheaper. But the train is faster and she can get more work done. So depending on how much time she has, Elana picks between saving time and saving money. To save many hours on the bus for himself, Morris Feldman (of Fayetteville fame) prefers to fly home to Arkansas from the University of Chicago. That's not a surprise, considering that it takes a whole lot of hours to get home by bus. But he knew months ahead of time that he'd be taking the bus home the summer after his sophomore year. Why? Because he'd spent a lot of money on his spring break trip and figured that taking the bus instead of flying would save him about $100.

Ride Boards

The cheapest way to travel is to scrounge a ride from someone else. Then your biggest expense is likely to be your share of the gas money and a stop for pizza. Get familiar with your school's ride board—a central bulletin board where students list rides that are offered and needed to various destinations—and check out if there are places in your school paper or on your school's web site that list rides. However, be careful whom you travel with. Always meet the person first and make sure you feel comfortable traveling with him or her.

Renting a Car

So you really want to take that road trip to New Orleans for Mardi Gras, but you can't wrestle the car away from your mom for an entire week. And you're just not so sure that your friend's jalopy can make the trip to New Orleans and back. So you decide to rent a car. Problem is, for students under the age of 25, it can be pretty hard to find a company that will rent to you. In New York, the Attorney General's office sued several car-rental companies for practicing age discrimination when they denied rentals based on age. As a result of a decision handed down in 1997, the companies do rent to young adults. But they can add an insurance surcharge for young drivers on top of the regular rental costs.

If you want to rent a car, you'll need to do a bit of hunting to see if you can find a company that will let you rent a car and give you a good deal. Here are some general tips:

- **Shop around.** Prices differ greatly. Besides varying by company, there are even differences within the same company. So ask each company you call if there's any way to lower the fee. Compare rates from several companies. And try to make a reservation ahead of time. As your trip gets closer, make another round of phone calls to see if prices have dropped. If so, you can make a new reservation and cancel your old one.

- **Ask about discounts.** See if you can use your AAA membership or your Student Advantage card. Check out discount coupons that you may receive with your credit card bills or frequent flier account statements. Read newspaper ads from rental companies promoting specials. Basically, you want to find any program that will take money off the basic cost of renting a car.

- **Ask about days of the week that are cheapest.** If you have a flexible schedule, you may be able to shave money off the price by switching to a less popular time.

- **Ask about price variations at pick-up and drop-off sites.** Prices will vary based on where you pick up and drop off the car. When you're checking out prices, ask about the cost difference between picking up at an airport versus getting a rental at a downtown location.

Rental companies tack on a lot of extra charges. Some that you're likely to see include:

- **Extra driver.** If you're hitting the road with a friend or two, make sure that each person who is going to drive is listed as a driver. You'll likely be charged a per diem or a flat rate for each extra driver. If you get in an accident and the person driving wasn't listed, the insurance company could claim that you didn't comply with the contract and refuse to pay.

- **Upgrades.** Why stick with a basic car if you could get all kinds of frills, including a fancier or more powerful car? Price, that's why. To keep your bill down, stick with the basics.

- **Insurance coverage.** It's critical to have insurance protection, but you don't need redundant coverage. Before you rent a car, check your auto insurance policy (if you have one) and your credit card coverage (you can call the 800 number listed on the back of the card) to see what kind of protection you already receive and when it kicks in. Gold credit cards and charge cards often give you collision damage insurance as one of your membership perks. If you're going to be renting a car while traveling abroad, be sure to make that clear to your insurance company and credit card issuer in case the coverage rules are different. Keep this information in mind as you are standing at the rental counter and the sales clerk is trying to convince you that you need to buy insurance coverage you may already have.

- **Fuel costs.** Be sure to fill the tank before you return a car. If you hand it in and it needs gas, you'll be charged some exorbitant rate. Also, don't buy the company's package to refuel the car when you return it. It's not worth it unless you're going to return the car on empty. Instead, fill up the tank yourself just before you get back to the rental counter.

Money Overseas

Before you take off for some foreign locale, call your bank to see if the ATM card you use to get cash at home can be used in cash machines where you will be traveling. If so, your ATM card can be the best way to get foreign currency. Many of the cash machines located around the globe are linked to the Cirrus and Plus networks that are common at home, so you can tap into them just as you do in the U.S. The best part of using your ATM card overseas is that you get the most favorable exchange rate that banks charge each other instead of the rate they normally give tourists. And don't worry if you've been sleeping through those 8 AM Spanish classes. When you insert your card in a foreign ATM the machines typically switch to English instructions. A few tips:

- Before you leave home, call your bank to find out if machines that accept your card are available where you'll be traveling. Ask the bank if it can send you a list of machine locations.

- Check with your bank to make sure you have the correct number of digits in your personal identification number. Some overseas ATM machines require a four-digit code, so if you currently have a five- or six-digit PIN, you'll need to switch it before you leave for your trip.

- Ask if you'll be charged a fee for withdrawing cash since you won't be using one of the machines in your bank's proprietary network. If so, you'll want to ration the number of trips you make to the ATM so you don't rack up a lot of unnecessary transaction charges.

- Make sure you have enough funds in your account so you can make all the withdrawals you're likely to need while traveling.

Cash machines also accept credit cards and let you access cash that way. But before you start withdrawing money this way, remember that getting cash from a credit card such as a Visa or MasterCard is considered a cash advance. You'll probably be charged a fee for the transaction, a high interest rate, and have interest charges start accruing just as soon as you withdraw the money. All these extras make cash advances a very expensive way to go. There are two ways to know the rules and fees for your specific credit card. You can read the terms of your account that you received when you first got your card (and I'm sure you know exactly where those are!) or you can call the 800 number that's listed on the back of your card and ask.

Do, however, use your credit card for purchases overseas. You'll get the same favorable exchange rate when you charge as you do when you use your ATM card to withdraw cash. Just make sure that you'll be home in time to pay the bill and that you have enough money to pay off all the purchases you make.

But don't rely totally on plastic. You'll want to carry some cash or a few traveler's checks with you just in case you can't find a machine that accepts your ATM card or you lose it. You can buy traveler's checks at a number of places, including banks, AAA offices, Thomas Cook outlets, and American Express Travel Service offices. Depending upon where you buy them, you may be charged about 1 percent or more of the total amount as a transaction fee. And you usually have to pay a transaction fee when you convert them into foreign currency. Since you'll be getting a less favorable exchange rate than you would when using an ATM or credit card, traveler's checks can be expensive to use.

Bon Voyage

Vacations can be a great relief from the stress of school and daily life. To get the most for your vacation dollar:

- **Don't go at peak times.** This way you'll get a better value when it comes to plane or train tickets, as well as lodging.

- **Stay in hostels.** They're cheaper than hotels. And you'll meet lots of interesting people.

- **Buy food in supermarkets and at outdoor markets.** Have a picnic and soak up the local scene. It's more relaxing—and cheaper—than eating in restaurants.

And have a great time!

Chapter

11

Investment Savvy

If you're like a lot of college students I know, you probably whiz right past the business section of the newspaper or, as I used to, throw the darn thing right in the trash. But if you think investing is only for finance or econ majors, think again. The world of business directly affects your pocketbook. And, practically speaking, banking recruiters often go for the lit majors, so it pays to know the basics just in case you decide to throw your post-graduation lot in with the Wall Street crowd.

This chapter is intended to give you a brief overview of investments. It won't cover all you need to know, but there are a number of good books that go into greater detail if you want to learn more. A good primer is *The Wall Street*

Journal Guide to Understanding Money & Investing. For useful definitions, check out Barron's *Dictionary of Finance and Investment Terms.*

It's the Economy, Stupid

James Carville made this phrase famous during the 1992 presidential campaign, when he encouraged Bill Clinton to focus on the state of the economy and avoid getting mired in other political tactics. Indeed, whether they are voting for a president or deciding how much to spend on vacation, Americans tend to follow their pocketbooks.

The state of the economy depends on a number of different components working in concert to operate smoothly. Over the past few years, we've had an unusual period of incredibly positive economic news, including:

- A strong stock market.
- Stable prices, meaning the cost of everything from bread to cars doesn't rise too quickly.
- Low unemployment.
- Wage growth, which means incomes aren't stagnant.
- Low interest rates that make it easy for consumers and corporations to borrow money to expand their business or buy a home.

There's no telling what state the economy will be in when you read this. In fact, there were warning signs in early 1998, namely instability in Asia, that could hurt the U.S. economy. There are a number of indicators that, whenever they occur, signal turbulent economic waters. Some to look out for:

- An overvalued stock market, where people bid up the share price of companies beyond what seems reasonable based on profit potential.
- Rising inflation, where the cost of goods rises quickly.

- Growing unemployment, where an increasing number of people are looking for work.

- Instability in a region of the world, such as Asia, where U.S. companies sell a lot of their goods.

Just how does all of this economic stuff affect you? When times are good, it will be easier for you to find work, make money, pay off your loans, and buy goods and services you need. When economic times are bad, it's harder to find work—and everything can spiral downhill from there. When I graduated from college, for example, there was a downturn in the economy, known as a recession, and jobs were hard to come by. I felt extremely lucky to get a job offer only a month or so after finishing a post-graduation summer job because newspapers were in the midst of laying off employees. A few years later, with the economy soaring, college graduates were having an easy time finding both employment and good salaries after graduation.

Whose Market is it Anyway?

There are two main ways to measure market performance, which generally refers to whether the price of stocks is rising or falling. The Dow Jones Industrial Average, a price-weighted average of 30 major companies, is the oldest and most widely used indicator of how the stock market performs. The Standard & Poor's 500 (better known as the S&P 500) tracks the market value of 500 large companies.

If the market is going up, the prices of the companies that make up these closely watched indicators are usually rising. When the market is falling, the companies that comprise these indexes are generally falling in value. As you can guess, these two ways of monitoring market activity aren't always accurate because they can't precisely reflect what's happened to each and every stock.

Stocks trade on various exchanges, such as the New York Stock Exchange, where many of the most established companies trade, and the NASDAQ, where a lot of technology companies trade. The exchanges are places where buyers and sellers come together on the trading floor in person, by phone, or via computer.

When people talk about overseas markets, they generally are referring to the performance of the major index of the country being discussed. For example, people follow the London FTSE and the Hong Kong Hang Seng.

Psychological Factors

The market is driven alternatively by greed and fear. People want to make money, but they also fear losing their shirts. In the short run, people overreact and the market can move in ways no rational person would guess. Over the long haul, however, economists have found the market to be very efficient, meaning stock prices reflect all information that is available about companies.

Sorting Out Stocks and Bonds

There are two basic kinds of financial assets, also known as securities: stocks and bonds.

- **Stocks are shares in corporations.** Each share of stock you or someone else owns represents part ownership in a company. The price of stock varies based on a number of factors. Among the most important are the expected earnings of the company, how popular the type of company is in the current economic climate, and how well the company's management runs business operations.

- **Bonds are debt.** When you buy a bond you are lending money to a company, government, or government agency in exchange for the promise of getting your money returned to you with interest. Bonds, also known as fixed-income securities, are affected by various factors, including how healthy the government or company is that issued it and how the interest rate it promised to pay compares to what the current market is paying.

Just How do You Buy Stocks and Bonds?

There are two main ways you can buy stocks and bonds:

- **Mutual funds.** You can pool your money with other investors who want to buy similar stocks or bonds in group-investment vehicles known as mutual funds. They are managed by professionals who get paid a percentage of all invested money to oversee the fund. No-load mutual funds do not charge you a sales fee to invest in the fund, while load funds tack on a sales charge either up-front or when you sell the investment.

Mutual funds come in any number of investment categories to reflect different styles of investing, from funds that invest in small companies that show potential to grow quickly to bonds issued by government agencies in a single state. Mutual funds that track either the entire market or a particular segment of the market are known as index funds. Funds where managers choose individual stocks or bonds in a quest to beat a particular segment of the market are known as actively managed funds.

Mutual funds help decrease your risk because they allow you to diversify your investments. If you have $1,000 to invest, for example, you would only be able to buy a limited number of shares in one or, at most, a handful of companies. With the same $1,000, you could invest in a mutual fund that holds a large basket of different securities, giving you the chance to diffuse the risk that one bad investment pick could send your total investment plummeting.

- **Brokerage account.** Consumers who buy stocks individually need to open a brokerage account from which they direct their investing. The people who execute purchase orders, also known as the trades, are brokers—middlemen that play matchmaker between people who want to buy particular shares and people who want to sell shares they own. Full-service brokers, like Merrill Lynch, charge a lot of money for each transaction and are expected to provide investment advice. Discount brokers, like Charles Schwab, provide less investment advice and charge lower fees. Increasingly, investors are trading online, where you get little to no personal advice, but can trade cheaply compared to the cost of using a real-live broker.

How You Make Money

With stocks, you make money in one of two ways:

- First, the company that issued the stock may pay a dividend, meaning it passes along part of its profits to shareholders. Shareholders get paid based on how many shares they own. You can cash in these payments or reinvest them and buy additional shares of the company. You pay taxes based on how much you earn from these dividends.

- The second way to make money is when the value of the stock climbs. These increases are known as capital gains. Say you buy shares in computer maker Compaq and the company announces that it made more money than it had expected and that it expects growth to continue at a healthy clip. People buying the stock are likely willing to pay a higher price for the stock than they would have before the announcement, so the company's stock price would likely rise. If you buy stock at $70 a share and sell it at $90 a share, you would make a profit of $20 a share. Of course, since nothing in this world is free, you'd be responsible for paying tax on the profit. And, just as you have a chance of seeing your stock price rise, it can also fall. If you sell for less than your purchase price, it's known as a capital loss.

With bonds, you can also make money in one of two ways.

- As we said, companies and governments that issue bonds agree to pay interest on your money. If you bought a bond for $100 that pays 5 percent and matures in one year, your investment would be worth $105 at the end of the year. Many people invest in bonds because it provides a steady income stream in the form of interest payments.

- The second way you make money explains the key to understanding bonds: When interest rates rise, the price of bonds falls. And when interest rates fall, the price of bonds rise. If, before the bond matures, interest rates fall and investors just getting into the market can only buy one-year bonds that pay 4 percent, the value of the investment we just talked about would rise and you could sell your bond early for a profit to someone who wants the opportunity to get paid 5 percent. But if interest rates rise and your bond now pays less than what new investors could get in the market, the value of your bond will fall. Still, you can hold on to it until it matures, when you should be able to collect the bond's face value plus the interest payment.

Cold, Hard Cash

We know cash as the green stuff that's hard to keep in our pocket. In investment terms, cash is a broader term to mean an investment that you can easily get your hands on without penalty and with little risk that its value will have fallen. It includes:

- Checking account.
- Passbook savings account.
- Money market account, which is an insured bank account that pays interest.

- Certificate of deposit (better known as a CD), which pays interest based on how long you leave your money on deposit. Terms typically range from one month to five years.

- Money market mutual fund, which invests in short-term bonds, certificates of deposit, and other cash investments that mature in less than a year. Money market funds are not insured, but are considered safe investments.

- Short-term bond fund, which invests in government and corporate bonds that mature within three years.

Cash investments are a way for people to keep money at their disposal while having different ways to maximize how much they earn on their investment. Rates vary widely depending on the type of investment. The average money market fund, for example, was paying 5.07 percent in March 1998, while the average interest-bearing checking account was paying only 1.52 percent.

Getting Started

Figuring out what types of investments you need or which are appropriate for your situation can be daunting. Most likely you have a checking account that may or may not be linked to a savings account at your bank. If your parents or grandparents have gotten you started in investing, you may have a money market fund or even some individual stocks. Where, if anywhere, do you go from here?

Let's be practical. As a student, you probably need at your disposal all the money you have. That means investing isn't a smart move for you now. You should consider stocks and bonds only when you are ready to move into longer-range investments, meaning money you won't need to rely on in the next three to five years.

When you do have money that you can think about investing, the cardinal rules are to make sure you match investments with your tolerance for risk and your time horizon. And it's important to remember that both stocks and bonds have risk factors. The following chart can help you pair your time horizon with your investment options.

Your Situation	Your Best options:
Need cash now	Checking account; savings account For more information: Bank Rate Monitor at www.bankrate.com
Want to earn a higher return on your money, but still need quick access	Bank money market account; money market mutual fund For more information: Bank Rate Monitor at www.bankrate.com; IBC Financial Data at www.ibcdata.com
Don't need money for a year or so and want to earn some extra money on your investment	Money market fund; short-term bond fund For more information: IBC Financial Data at www.ibcdata.com; Morningstar at www.morningstar.net
Don't need money for three years	Short- or intermediate-term bond fund For more information: Morningstar at www.morningstar.net
Don't need money for more than three years and are willing to take some risks	Mutual fund that tracks a particular index, such as an S&P 500 fund For more information: Morningstar at www.morningstar.net
Have been studying the market and are ready to take on even more risk	Mutual funds, either index or actively managed; individual stocks For more information: Morningstar at www.morningstar.net; Yahoo at www.quote.yahoo.com; The Motley Fool at www.fool.yahoo.com

Slow and Steady

You may have some hot shot friends who brag about their investments and talk about how much money they're making in the stock market. The only people who get rich quickly in the stock market, however, are those individuals who place big bets and are extremely, and we mean extremely, lucky. Slow and steady not only wins the race, it saves you the heartache of losing money unnecessarily.

Before you invest in anything, ask yourself these five questions:

- **Do I know what transaction costs are involved?** If you're considering a mutual fund, for example, ask yourself what sales charge you would need to pay and if you've looked for no-load funds that would meet your investment criteria. There are so many great no-load funds out there that you'd be hard pressed to come up with a reason to buy a fund with a load.

- **How much risk is involved?** You want to know how much money you could potentially earn and how much you could potentially lose. If you're investing in a stock or bond fund, for example, ask the company that manages the fund what the fund's worst one-year performance has been.

- **How easily can I sell the investment if I need to get my money out?** Bank certificates of deposit, for example, usually make you pay a penalty fee if you withdraw your money early. And remember, the more obscure the investment, the harder it will be to sell. Investments that are easy to touch are known as liquid investments.

- **Will the investment help you reach a specific goal, such as saving for a car or investing for a graduate degree?** Again, you want to pair your investment goal with the type of investment you choose. If you need your money for law school tuition that is due in two years, for example, you don't want to put it in the stock market where you may be forced to sell into a declining market.

- **Have you done your homework and researched the investment?** Remember to use objective, not subjective criteria. Sure you may love the sneakers you wear and want to invest in the company that makes them. But does the company have a lot of debt? Have its sales been growing or shrinking? The best way to keep informed about companies and markets is to read *The Wall Street Journal*.

Chapter 12

Reality Strikes

Whether you're about to graduate or you're just thinking ahead, the sad truth is that reality eventually settles in. You have to pay taxes (sometimes even when you're in school). And you have to pay off the debt you've taken on to finance your college degree. This chapter gives you a few words of advice and encouragement about handling the cold, harsh world of adult responsibility. Just hang in there, and you'll see that you can deftly maneuver through the maze of sobering topics like taxes and student loans. Who knows? You may even be able to use this advice at a party and dazzle your friends with your wisdom when these topics come up for discussion.

The Tax Man Cometh

Your least favorite uncle is probably named Sam. Instead of being a kindly old fart who gives you inexplicably large birthday gifts, this one wants your cold, hard cash. And with what seems like more laws than you have hair on your head, he wants to confuse you more often that he wants to offer clarity.

I'll walk you through a few of the tax laws that directly affect you. But realize that tax rules change as often as the wind shifts direction. And there are numerous laws that apply to each person's personal situation. So while the information here is current as of this writing, it is not exhaustive and it may not be fresh when you sit down to use it. Janice Johnson, a New York-based tax expert, says it's important to check tax information every year before you file your return. There are tax law changes when Congress updates the rules. And there are regular adjustments made to various dollar amounts based on inflation.

There are lots of ways you can stay current. Newspapers always write about major tax changes. The Internal Revenue Service has an extensive web site where you can look up information on the current tax code and download any publications and federal tax forms that you need (www.irs.ustreas.gov). There are numerous books that are sold every tax season, a period that runs from the beginning of each calendar year through April 15, when tax returns, the forms you need to file, are due to the IRS and your state government. And there are retail software programs that walk you, step by step, through the maze of filling out that current year's tax forms. The most popular programs are Intuit's TurboTax (the Macintosh version is called MacIntax) and Kiplinger TaxCut. There's no need to be a tax martyr. If you need help getting answers to tax questions and you can't find the answer in one of the references I mentioned above, ask a friend, relative, or tax professional.

Check out IRS publications or tax books to see if, however, you even need to file a return, a decision that is based on various criteria, such as your age and income. If, however, you had federal taxes withheld from your paycheck and are due a refund, you'll need to file a return even if you don't meet the minimum filing requirements. Taxes are withheld from your paycheck based on information you give on what's known as a W-4 form, which you fill out each time you start a job.

Tax Status of Scholarships and Grants

As mentioned in chapter 1, any scholarship or grant money that you receive over and above the cost of tuition, fees, books, supplies, and equipment that is required for your courses is taxable. So you'll have to pay taxes on any extra funds that you get for food, transportation, or general living expenses. The good news is that in 1997 Congress passed a series of tax breaks for students and their families. Among the highlights:

- **Interest deductions for student loans.** You'll be able to deduct interest payments on student loans that are due and paid after December 31, 1997. You can use the deduction during the first 60 months of repaying your loans. The maximum deduction is $1,000 in 1998, $1,500 in 1999, $2,000 in 2000, and $2,500 in 2001 and beyond. What does this mean for you? If in the year 2000 you pay off part of your student loan, including $1,000 in interest, you can deduct $1,000 from your income. This lowers your total taxable income and cuts the amount you need to pay in taxes. The interest rate deduction is phased out for single people who earn between $40,000 and $55,000 or more. (Married people filing a joint return lose the benefit if they make more than $75,000.)

- **The Hope scholarship.** This tax credit gives taxpayers up to $1,500 directly off the amount they owe in taxes for each student they support in each of the first two years of a post-secondary education. The credit can be used for amounts spent on tuition and fees.

Paying Off Student Loans

Before you graduate, you'll have an exit interview with your school's financial aid office. You'll discuss your student loans—from how much you owe to your various repayment options. As I said in chapter 1, this book won't give you a comprehensive guide to financing the cost of your college education or to paying off your student loans. It will, however, give you key points to keep in mind as you approach repaying. You can refer to the first chapter and to the appendix for suggestions on where to find additional information on the topic.

The good news: You don't have to pay back the money all at once. Federal student loans are typically repaid over a ten-year period. And student loans have a grace period before your first payments are due. You won't have to start paying off your subsidized or unsubsidized Stafford loans, for example, until six months after you graduate. (Remember, with subsidized loans the government pays the interest payments on your loan until six months after you graduate.) Perkins loans will come due six to nine months after graduation.

All this means that you have some time to figure out what you're doing after graduation, get a job, and set up a budget that includes your monthly student loan payments. And you will definitely need to set up a budget. If you're like the typical student who graduates owing $11,500 in student loans, you can expect to pay $139 a month if you are paying off your loans over a ten-year period at 8 percent. The total borrowing cost by the time you're done repaying: $16,743.

Your loan may have been sold by your original lender to a company whose business is to buy and service student loans. So instead of paying back the lender that gave you the loan, you'll make your payments to one of these companies, such as NellieMae or SallieMae. After you graduate, you'll get a notice from the servicer that tells you when you need to start paying your loan and how much your monthly payments will be.

What do you have to do? Make your payments on time; let your lender know if you move, change your name or get a new Social Security number; and, if you can't make your regular payments, ask for a deferment (when you get permission to postpone repayment for such situations such as returning to school) or a forbearance (a temporary change to your repayment terms in cases where you have a financial hardship and can't handle the regular payments).

Okay, so now that reality has set in, here are some tips for paying off your student loans:

- **Repayment options.** Companies offer various methods for paying off your student loans. If you're like most students, you'll pick a straight-forward repayment plan where you spread out your loan payments in equal installments over ten years. If you can't afford that, you may opt for a plan that lets you pay less during the early years and step up payments as you earn more money. Bear in mind that nothing is free. If you pay less early on, you'll end up paying more over the life of the loan because you end up borrowing the money for a longer period of time. Before you pick a repayment option, consider what you can afford now in monthly payments and your total costs over the life of the loan.

- **Pay on time.** Not only will you avoid running into problems that can be reported to credit reporting agencies, but you may qualify for certain breaks available to borrowers who have built a solid payment history. SallieMae, for example, cuts the interest rate of Stafford loans by two percentage points for borrowers who make their first 48 payments on time. Over a ten-year re-payment period, someone who borrows $20,000 at the current interest rate of 8.25 percent would save $1,156. NellieMae gives borrowers an option to have the rate of their Stafford loans cut by two percentage points after they've made the first 48 payments on time or have NellieMae pay their last six scheduled monthly loan payments.

- **Consider having payments taken directly from your bank account.** Some companies cut the interest rate of your loan, say by a quarter of a point, if you have the payments directly debited from your checking or savings account. This method will save you good money over the life of the loan. And since you know ahead of time exactly how much money will be deducted from your account, you can monitor the activity.

- **If you move or change your name, let your loan servicer know.** That way, you will get all the mail it sends you about your loans. Plus, the lender knows where to find you if there's a problem with your account.

- **If you run into problems, call your lender.** You may be able to ask for a special program that lets you defer payment or somehow avoid going into default on your loan. "Don't run away from us if you have trouble. Come to us," says Scott Miller, the former director of government relations for SallieMae. "There's a lot we can do to help."

- **Consider consolidating your loans.** If you owe at least $7,500 through federal student loan programs, look into combining your various loans into one, if the program allows. If you have too many loans to keep track of or feel like you're crumbling under the weight of repaying them, consolidation can help you cut your monthly payments by stretching out the repayment period. But realize that any program that gives you lower monthly payments adds to your total borrowing costs.

- **Read your mail.** That's the only way you'll know if your loan is sold to another company. You'll also find out if there is a problem. It may not make the most scintillating reading, but it's the only way you'll have all the information you need to handle your account.

- **Reach out and call someone.** If you have questions, you can probably find the answer by calling NellieMae (800-367-8848) or SallieMae (888-272-5543).

If you stay disciplined and focused, you'll make a dent in your loan payments and will eventually get to the point where you can breathe a deep sigh of relief—you'll have completely paid off your loans.

Chapter 13

Frequently Asked Questions about Personal Finance

This chapter covers common questions you're likely to have about money. The answers will give you tips to maneuver through the consumer world with grace and knowledge. Some of the topics have been covered in previous chapters, others are new. So, go ahead, peruse all those questions you've been dying to ask: Just what is the difference between a credit card and a charge card? Why does my money earn so little in the bank? And, perhaps most importantly, can I get rich quick?

If Money Doesn't Grow on Trees, Where Will I Get It?

I want to make some extra money during the semester, but don't have the motivation to find a job. What should I do?

You're going to need to pick yourself up and look. Lucky for you, businesses near college campus are used to dealing with people who have weird schedules. Stop by local stores, like the ice cream shop near your dorm, and ask if they are hiring. Check out bulletin boards around campus for job postings. See if your school's Internet site has an employment section. Stop by your financial aid and career services offices to see what job listings they have. Also, don't forget to check out the classified ads in your campus paper, as well as the town's local paper.

I'm worried about what job I'll get after college and whether I'll be able to pay off my student loans. What should I do?

Definitely make an appointment to meet with a career counselor on campus. Also, see if your school as an alumni job network. You may be able to do short internships with alums who work in fields where you have an interest. If you're graduating with a lot of debt, you will need to look for a job that will provide a decent enough salary that you can support yourself and pay off your loans. You also may want to scope out some of the online job search tools to get a sense of what resources are available on the Internet and what jobs are currently being offered. Check out: College Grad Job Hunter at www.collegegrad.com and The Monster Board at www.monster.com. Don't stress too much, however. You're asking the right questions at the right time. Keep an eye toward the future in terms of what jobs you're interested in and what you're qualified for. But try not to let stress take away from the enjoyment of your college years.

How Not to Run Out of Money

My friends and I order in a lot of food. Is this a bad habit?

Even if you're Julia Child, it's nice to have a night off from cooking. But ordering in gets expensive. And, unless you have a very generous amount of money to spend each month, you're probably spending more money than you should on food. Say you and your roommates order in from the local Chinese restaurant. You'll probably spend about $20 for three of you. Take that $20 to the grocery store and you could buy enough food to get you through several meals. It's okay to order in food. And many a cramming session calls for a pizza. But it is important to try to limit how often you order in and what you chose to order on those occasions. Pizza, for example, is a lot less expensive than sushi.

How can I cut down my grocery bill?

There are several strategies you can use to get out of the supermarket spending less money than you may now. Cut down on buying prepared and packaged foods. Buy as much as possible in bulk. Look for store brands of products. And buy lots of fresh fruits and vegetables that are in season. Sure it's tempting to buy some fabulous sun-dried tomato gourmet ravioli, and prepared tomato sauce. But for a whole lot less money, you can buy a can of crushed tomatoes and fresh vegetables to make your own sauce. If you like to have coffee every day, stock up on good coffee you can make at home and pour it in a cup you can take to class. Like to start the day with a bagel and cream cheese? If you buy your own cream cheese and keep a dozen bagels in the freezer, you'll cut down on those $1.75 runs to the local bagel shop.

My school requires me to sign up for a meal plan, but I can't stand eating in the cafeteria.

A lot of schools now give students options. Some schools even let you use points from your meal plan at an on-campus fast-food restaurant, café, or market. Be sure to check with your school's dining services to see what the minimum plan requirement is, as well as all your options for using your pre-paid plan.

Banking 101

What are the different kind of banks?

Banks come in three major styles—commercial banks, savings and loans, and credit unions. Commercial banks originally dealt with corporations, but have moved increasingly into the consumer market, where they now offer checking and savings accounts, credit cards, auto loans, student loans, and mortgages for home purchases. Savings and loans, also known as thrifts, focus mostly on the consumer market. Home loans used to be their bread and butter, but after they expanded into other areas many of them ran into financial problems. Many closed. Others consolidated or merged into commercial banks. You can still find some good deals on checking accounts at the remaining savings and loans. Credit unions are made up of members who have a common bond, such as the same employer or same school. Credit unions are nonprofit institutions and, therefore, have some great deals for their members. Credit unions usually have checking accounts that require lower minimum balance requirements and loans that have better interest rates than you can find at large commercial banks. If you are eligible to join a credit union, definitely check out what accounts and services would be available to you—and at what price.

My bank slaps me with a fee when I ask for a simple service. What's the deal?

There's no limit on how much money banks can charge you for their service fees. They also aren't restricted by what services they can charge you for. So, in essence, a bank can charge you for anything from copying canceled checks to holding your mail while you're on vacation. If you are a good customer of your bank, meaning you do a fair amount of business and pay your bills on time, ask it to waive whatever fees you think are unreasonable. If you don't ask or the bank says no, unfortunately, you're stuck with the bill. The good news is that banks are required to inform you of any new charges or increased service fees, so check out whatever mail your bank sends to you. Yes, that even means reading the fine print of the notices that are enclosed with your monthly statement. Forewarned is forearmed.

How long after it's written can a check be cashed?

It depends. Banks must make a good-faith effort to make sure any older checks they cash are truly good. And in most states, a stop-payment order that's placed on a check is good for only six months.

How long does it take for a check to clear?

You can access money from both cash and checks you deposit on the next business day after you make the deposit. There are, of course, a few exceptions: Banks can take two days to credit a cashier's check that's written for more than $5000, and five days if a check you deposit is drawn on an out-of-state bank.

What protections do I have when I make a deposit at the ATM?

Banks generally have two employees process deposits that are made at ATMs. And banks are required to investigate any claims from consumers that a mistake was made. If you deposit a check and have a problem, you can always trace the paper trail created by the check back to the person or company that issued it in the first place. But if you deposit cash, and the bank claims the deposit wasn't made, it's most likely going to come down to your word against the bank's. Personally, I don't deposit cash at an ATM. Why take the chance?

Why do I earn so little on my deposits?

Good question. The answer comes from a combination of factors. Right now, interest rates are relatively low on both deposits and loans. When interest rates do rise, banks are likely to move the rates they charge for their loans more quickly than they move the rates they pay out for money consumers deposit at the bank. Finally, when loan demand is relatively low, banks don't have a great incentive to pay higher rates that would attract money to the bank that they could then turn around and lend out to individuals or companies for a higher rate. All in all, you can be sure you'll pay more to borrow money from a bank than you'll earn on your deposits.

The World of Plastic

What's the difference between a credit card and a charge card?

A charge card is a piece of plastic from a lender who expects you to pay off your purchases within a month of receiving your bill. A credit card represents a loan or a line of credit from a lender. Each month, you receive a bill for the purchases you made over the past month. You can pay off the balance in full or revolve part of the balance into the future. You must pay interest on any money that you don't pay off by the time the bill is due. Interest rates are usually high, on average about 18 percent. And you get socked not only on interest charges if you don't pay off your bill in full, but can also rack up charges if you send in your monthly payment late or charge more than the total credit limit that's been allocated to you.

Why do some stores and restaurants say you have to spend a certain amount of money before you can use your credit card?

Stores have to pay credit card companies a transaction fee for each purchase that consumers make, so many stores don't like when you charge very small amounts. But Visa and MasterCard, which are both associations of banks that issue credit cards, prohibit merchants from setting minimum purchase requirements because these associations don't want to discourage consumers from charging. American Express also discourages storeowners from setting a minimum. When you're at a store that says it has a minimum, tell the clerk the store's not allowed to do that. If he or she doesn't care what you say and still refuses to accept your credit card, you should call the company that issued your card and complain.

I recently received a credit card in the mail that I didn't request. To activate the card, I have to call a toll-free number. Am I responsible for this card?

Credit card companies are not allowed to send people credit cards they have not requested. What they can do is send out replacement cards when old cards expire. Say you have a propriety gas card. The company can decide to replace its existing cards with a co-branded Visa or MasterCard. If you didn't request the card and it's not a replacement for some other card you carry, you shouldn't be responsible if someone else gets his hands on the card and racks up charges. Still, it's a good idea to call the issuer and make sure the account is closed and can't be activated. This can save you a lot of headaches down the road.

I settled a credit card debt with a collection agency by paying less than the full amount I owed. Can they put information on my credit report?

In short, yes. Even though the debt collector (on behalf of the lender) accepted less than your full payment, it is entitled to tell the credit reporting agencies of the deal. Since you were late in your payments and didn't pay the full amount you owed, the information will remain on your credit report for seven years. You can, however, add your own statement to explain any extenuating circumstances that required you to pay less then the total. And you should do this if something like a major illness or losing a job prevented you from staying current on your account.

Payback Time

I feel like I'm drowning under a pile of bills. What should I do?

The first step you can take to help get your situation under control is to stop buying new things so that you can concentrate on paying off current bills and any debt you've accumulated. Write down a list of all the money you owe, whether it's to parents, friends, or credit card companies. Then write down the interest rate you pay for each loan. Call each credit card lender to whom you owe money and ask if it will lower the interest rate you're being charged. Each month, make sure you pay at least the minimum amount due on each loan. Plus, send in as much above the minimum required payment as you can afford to the credit card with the highest interest rate. As soon as you're done paying off that loan, send the amount you've been paying to the loan with the next highest interest rate. If you feel like you can't handle the problem yourself, call a local office of the National Foundation for Consumer Credit, a nonprofit organization that offers credit-counseling services nationwide. Call 800-388-2227 to be referred to an office near you, where you can meet with a counselor who will help you set up a budget and a debt repayment plan.

How do I know if I have too much debt?

First of all, as a student you should separate the loans you take out to pay for your education from other loans like credit cards or money you borrow from friends to buy a concert ticket. Student loans are like an investment. You borrow money so you can get an education that will set you on a career path that not only makes you happy, but also enables you to do something useful with your life and make enough money to support yourself in adulthood. Credit card debt is not an investment, but rather a means of paying for items you buy along the way. Ideally, you should spend no more than you can afford to pay off each month. In reality, people rack up debt, buying anything from Christmas presents for their friends to plane tickets for a European adventure to the latest bestseller. Here's one way to look at it: When you're older and ready to buy a house, lenders recommend that you spend no more than 28 percent of your income on your housing expenses, and no more than a total of 36 percent of your income for all consumer debt—that includes any loans you take out to buy a house, pay for college, finance a car, or put on your credit card.

A Roof Over Your Head

I want to live off campus, but am not sure if I can afford it. What extra expenses will I have?

Besides rent, you can expect to pay for utilities (electricity, gas, and in some cases, water), your telephone bill (that includes the monthly cost of having phone service, as well as what you'll spend on long-distance calls), the cost of furnishing the place, and food. Don't underestimate the cost of furniture. Sure you can buy plastic milk crates for little money. But if you don't have a bed or a stitch of furniture, you're going to need to cough up some bucks to fill the place. You should also expect to put down one or two months of rent as a security deposit the landlord can have if you leave damage behind after you move out, as well as your first or last month's rent. And if you're not covered under your parents' insurance, you should get a renter's insurance policy that covers your apartment for loss, damage, and liability.

What happens if I miss a rent payment?

Worst case scenario, you can get kicked out of your apartment. If you are going to be a few days late paying the rent, call your landlord and explain the problem. Tell him the earliest you can get him the money. If you have a good excuse and a good landlord, you can expect a little leeway. But if you fall behind, you can also find yourself being evicted from your apartment.

Smart Shopping

Why is it so expensive to own a car?

Besides paying for the car itself, you'll need to pay for gas (which is always more expensive than you think), insurance (a must), and repairs (which need to be made all too often). Think that little rattle can be ignored? Not after you speak to your mechanic who says it's dangerous to drive your car in its present condition. And that will be $500, thank you very much. No matter how you slice it, cars are an expensive proposition. So before you take the plunge, sit down with a parent or someone else who's owned a car and go over what you can realistically expect to spend for the privilege of owning four wheels.

Does it pay to shop around for gas?

Put it this way. I live in New York City, where the local gas station charges well over $1.50 a gallon for gas. Near my office in Yonkers, I pay closer to $1.26. That's a difference of several dollars each time I fill up, so I'm careful to fill up the tank outside of Manhattan. If you work at a job that pays minimum wage, you could be talking about close to an extra hour of work just to fill the tank.

Do I pay the same prices no matter where I shop?

Generally, you pay for convenience. So the on-campus or local store may charge more for something than what you'd pay for the same thing at a discount store located a few miles outside the center of town. Lucky for all of us, it's a great time to be a consumer. There are so many discount stores, outlet malls, and giant warehouse stores where you can find cut-rate prices. One recent example: I just had a party for a friend and wanted to serve brunch type of food. I bought a big package of smoked salmon at Costco, a warehouse store where I pay a $35 annual fee to be able to shop at any of its stores. The package cost me $15.99 for a pound and a half of the fish. At a small store near my apartment, I'd probably pay close to $30 for the same amount of food.

I think I have a shopping problem. I can't always afford what I buy, but I can't stop myself from buying. What should I do?

There are a few strategies you can try. First of all, don't go into stores that tempt you. Second, take a friend with you when you do go shopping and ask him or her to help you keep your impulse purchases to a minimum. Third, don't carry a checkbook or credit card with you when you go to a store. That way, you can't buy anything more expensive than you have the cash for. Finally, carry a small notebook with you and write down any purchases you are considering. Leave the store and rest on the decision a few days. If after a few days you still want to make the purchase and can afford it, at least you'll have made a well-thought out choice. If these aren't enough to help you curb your spending and you suspect you need help with your problem, call your school's psychological services office and set up an appointment to speak with a counselor. Sometimes excessive shopping may be hiding other problems.

Healthy Choices

I don't have health insurance and I don't want to spend the money to get coverage. How important is it?

If you're smart, you'll sign up right away. Walking around without health insurance is like taking one big, continuous risk. If you get sick or injured, you'll have to pay all of your medical bills out of your own pocket. That can get expensive. And don't think you can avoid payment. Even if you wanted to, which we'd hope you wouldn't, it's not so easy to walk away from these bills. A doctor or hospital will probably go to collections, meaning they hire a company to come after you for payment. And any bad debts can be recorded on your credit report.

I'm about to graduate from school and I don't yet have a job. How can I get medical insurance?

If you're not still covered under a parent's policy, you may be able to pay to continue coverage from their plan under COBRA, a federal program that, among other things, requires companies with more than 20 employees to extend coverage of a child who is no longer considered a dependent under the policy and doesn't qualify for another group health plan. Otherwise, look into getting a short-term major medical policy. These plans typically have a high deductible and don't cover routine care. But they're great protection against being devastated by the cost of a major illness.

Fun in the Sun

What's the best way to get money when traveling?

If you have an ATM card that's linked to one of the major networks of cash machines like Cirrus or Plus, you can retrieve money almost anywhere in the country, and in many places around the globe. Using your ATM card is convenient and, if you're traveling overseas, makes it easy to get local currency at the best exchange rate. When you travel overseas, remember to check with your bank before you take off for your trip to make sure your card and personal identification number will work in machines wherever you'll be traveling. Your PIN will need to be a certain number of digits in some countries, so you may need to change it from the current one. Also, be sure to ask what fees, if any, you'll be charged for using a machine that doesn't belong to your bank.

Can I get special discounts as a student?

Pile them on. As a student, you're entitled to a host of discounts that range from cheaper museum admissions to cut-rate airline tickets. Wherever you go and whatever reservations you book, be sure to mention that you're a student and see if there are any special price breaks. Also, look into getting an international student ID card that will open up even more special deals. Sometimes you may wish you were out "in the real world," but there are no student discounts when you trade in your full load of courses for a full-time job.

Why is it so hard for someone my age to rent a car?

Younger drivers get in more accidents than do drivers with more years of experience under their belt. So car rental companies try to protect themselves from bigger loses by limiting the age consumers need to be before they can rent a car. Some states, however, prohibit this discrimination. So if you need to rent a car, definitely call around to various rental companies and see what they offer. If you think you're being discriminated against, call your local consumer protection office or state attorney general's office, whose number can be found in the blue pages of your phone book.

I really want to go away for Spring Break, but am not sure I can afford it. What are my options?

One of the most important lessons about dealing with your personal finances is to be realistic about what you can afford to do and what you can't afford to do. No matter what your personal situation, chances are you have friends who have more money than you do, as well as friends who have less money than you do. You'll save yourself heartache and the hassle of committing to spending money you don't have, if you do only those activities you can afford. That may mean you can't go away for Spring Break. Or it may mean talking to your friends about finding a trip you can all afford. You may all decide to go hiking and camping at a nearby mountain, for example, instead of flying off to Florida for a week on the beach. Or you may decide to work extra hours to earn the money you need to pay for the trip. Another option is to see if you can work for the company that is selling one of the packages you're interested in. In exchange, you may get some kind of price break.

I'm not sure what is considered a proper tip. Can you give me some guidelines?

The most common place to leave a tip is in a restaurant, where the accepted practice is to leave between 15 and 20 percent of the pre-tax bill. Tips are meant to reward good service, so you should base the amount you leave on how good the service was. If you have a terrible waiter who paid no attention to you, you may want to leave a small tip or nothing at all. If the service was out of this world (and you can afford it), you may want to head toward the 20 percent range. Other common places to tip include taxi cabs, where you generally give about 10 to 15 percent of the fare; parking garages, where you tip $1 to the attendant who retrieves your car; and hotels, where you tip about $1 per bag to bell men and about $2 to $5 a night to the housekeeper. And, at holiday time, remember that tips are expected to thank those people who provided you with various services during the past year. Hint: This will also encourage them to look out for you in the coming months. These people include superintendents and doormen in an apartment building, the person who cuts your hair regularly, and the person who delivers your newspaper. If you're going to be traveling overseas, check out a guidebook to see what the local tipping customs are in such places as restaurants and on guided tours. In some countries, for example, the local custom is to leave only whatever additional loose change you have after paying the bill.

Investment Savvy

What's the difference between a stock and a bond?

Stock is a share in a company. Bonds are debt issued by a company or a government. If you buy 10 shares of stock in company XYZ, for example, you would then own a piece of that company, however small. Your percentage of ownership would depend on the total number of shares the company has issued. Stocks trade on exchanges where buyers and sellers are paired based on market demand and price. Bonds represent money you are lending to a company, government, or government agency in exchange for a promise to get your money back with interest. Say you invest $1,000 in the debt of company XYZ. The company agrees to pay back your $1,000 within a certain period of time, as well as pay you a certain interest rate, say 7 percent a year, for the use of your money.

What is a mutual fund?

A mutual fund is an investment vehicle that pools money from various individuals or companies and invests the funds in a particular asset class or using a certain investment style. Stock funds, for example, invest in the stocks of various kinds of companies. Bond funds invest in corporate and/or government debt. Money market funds invest in cash investments, such as bank certificates of deposit and short-term bonds that mature within a year. Index funds are mutual funds that are designed to match the performance of a particular segment of the market or the entire market. Funds have different investment styles. A stock fund, for example, may invest in small company growth stocks, meaning those small companies that are believed to have good potential to grow larger and earn more money. Bond funds may invest in bonds issued by companies, the U.S. government, or emerging-market countries.

What is a mutual fund company?

A mutual fund company is a company that offers an array of mutual funds. Some mutual fund companies whose names you would recognize include Fidelity, Vanguard, and T. Rowe Price.

Can I get rich quickly?

Sure, and you can retire tomorrow. Remember, investments that have higher returns usually mean you must take on more risk. When it comes to investing, only the rare (and extremely lucky) person gets rich quickly.

Am I too young to invest?

You're never too young to start investing and to start learning about markets. Most likely, as a student, you don't have much extra money to get started. But you shouldn't automatically rule out investing. Whatever you do, start slowly. Say you have $3,000 saved from a summer job. Consider putting the money in a money market fund instead of a bank savings account. While money market funds don't have the same federal insurance as bank deposit accounts, they are considered to be a safe investment. And by putting your money in a money market fund you can earn more interest than you would in a bank savings account. And you can get your feet wet as you move into the investment world.

How can I learn more about investing?

If they're knowledgeable, start by asking your parents or older siblings to explain some of the basics to you. My dad, for example, loves to talk about the stock market and mutual funds, so nothing would make him happier than to sit down for an hour and answer questions. You may also be able to take some kind of class at school. It's also a great idea to start reading the business section of your newspaper, where you can read about stocks, bonds, and the economy. There are also a number of good books that explain the basics. To stay informed, nothing beats reading *The Wall Street Journal*.

Reality Strikes

How do I know if I must file a tax return?

Whether you need to file a tax return or not depends on much money you've made during the year and if you've had money withheld from a paycheck. Pick up a current copy of this year's tax forms, which spell out who must file. You can find the forms at public libraries and at the Post Office. You can also download tax forms and instructions from the IRS at www.irs.ustreas.gov. Even if you don't meet the minimum filing requirements but have had money withheld from a paycheck, you'll likely need to file a tax return so you can get back whatever money is due to you. Remember, if you have to file, you'll need to file both a federal and a state return.

Where can I get help with my taxes?

You probably have a very simple tax return that requires you to report only your wage income and look up your tax liability in the tax tables. With your income, you'll likely qualify to fill out a 1040 EZ, a one-page tax return that you can easily complete using the instructions that are included. If you have income from investments or other complex issues to figure out, consider using one of the two main tax software packages on the market—TurboTax by Intuit or Kiplinger TaxCut by Block Financial. These programs guide you through filling out your return by walking you through an interview session. You answer the questions the program asks, and it fills in all the necessary forms. There are commercial services that will do your taxes for a fee, but again, you probably have a straightforward return and can handle it on your own.

How much money should I give to charity? And how do I know if an organization is legitimate?

Giving to charities is worthwhile and fulfilling. But remember, as a student, you probably can't afford to be as generous as you'd like—or as generous as you can be once you're fully immersed in the working world. So if you can't afford to give money or want to supplement how much you can afford to donate, you can always give your time. Volunteering is much needed and much appreciated. In terms of finding out about individual organizations, there are a few places you can get information. On the Internet, check out GuideStar at www.guidestar.org for information about various groups. To get information by mail: You can get a copy of *"Wise Giving Guide"* from the National Charities Information Bureau by writing to the organization at 19 Union Square West, New York, New York 10003. For *"Give But Give Wisely"* from the Philanthropic Advisory Service, send a self-addressed stamped envelope to Holiday Giving, Council of Better Business Bureaus, 4200 Wilson Boulevard, Suite 800, Arlington, Virginia 22203-1804. And for the American Institute of Philanthropy's *"Charity Rating Guide & Watchdog Report,"* write to American Institute of Philanthropy, 4905 DelRay Avenue, Suite 300, Bethesda, Maryland 20814. It costs $3.

Conclusion

The Buck Stops Here

So, you've survived Psych 101. You've had more than your fair share of macaroni and cheese in your school's dining hall. And you've negotiated sharing only one phone with a roommate. We hope this book has helped with a few of the financial twists and turns you've hit along the way—like figuring out how to get a cheap plane ticket so you can join your friends for a spring break trip and dealing with your first big credit card bill. No doubt, there will be some tight times along the way when your life would be much easier if you had the financial resources of Oprah Winfrey. But remember, even Oprah was once a struggling college student. Armed with all your new knowledge about money matters, you can take charge of your financial life. As we said in the introduction, you'll be able to stave off debt and starvation. You're in control.

Appendix

The following is a list of sources for additional information on topics covered in the book. It is by no means exhaustive, and the descriptions given are brief.

General information about personal finance:

The following monthly magazines each carry a wealth of information on a range of consumer topics:

Consumer Reports

Kiplinger's

Money

SmartMoney

College applications, student loans, and scholarships:

The College Board at www.collegeboard.org

> Useful features include information about college costs and a scholarship search engine.

The U.S. Department of Education at www.ed.gov

> This government site includes the most recent *Student Guide,* which has information about financial aid.

FastWEB at www.fastweb.com

> This is a free scholarship search engine that boasts a database of over 400,000 scholarships.

The Financial Aid Information Page at www.finaid.org

> This site is chock full of great information and links to other useful sites. It is managed by financial aid expert Mark Kantrowitz. The site includes calculators for projecting future college costs, loan comparisons, and an undergraduate student loan advisor. Check out Mark's favorite related sites at www.finaid.org/finaid/picks.html

NellieMae's site at www.nelliemae.org

> The organization offers tips on preparing for college and information on ordering its free publications, including *Be a Wise Borrower* and *Student Loan Advisor.*

Peterson's College Guide at www.petersons.com

> Offerings include a glossary of financial aid terms and a helpful question-and-answer section on financial aid.

The Princeton Review at www.review.com

> Offers a range of information for college students and prospective students.

Sallie Mae's site at www.SallieMae.com

> This site has helpful advice on topics like forecasting college costs and estimating borrowing needs. It also includes tips on shopping and applying for financial aid.

Banking, credit cards, and debt management:

In general, many banks have extensive proprietary sites that have details about their account offerings, as well as general personal finance information. Use a search engine to find a bank you are interested in or try using a bank's proper name, such as www.bankamerica.com or www.firstunion.com

Bank Rate Monitor at www.bankrate.com

> The site provides information on fees and interest rates, as well as articles on banking and credit cards.

Banxquote at www.banxquote.com

> You can find interest rate information, general personal finance advice, and links to related sites.

CheckFree at www.checkfree.com

> For information on electronic bill paying.

Debt Counselors of America at www.dca.org

> This site has numerous booklets that you can download.

Financenter at www.financenter.com

> Check out the financial calculators.

Kiplinger's at www.kiplinger.com

> The personal finance magazine offers financial calculators and a library of its past stories.

The National Foundation for Consumer Credit at www.nfcc.org

> The organization offers general information about debt, as well as referrals to a Consumer Credit Counseling Service office near you.

Nolo at www.nolo.com

> This publisher of legal and consumer information offers a "legal encyclopedia" of debt and credit terms.

Quicken at www.quicken.com

For information on online banking and bill paying.

For a list of low-rate credit cards:

> Card Web
>
> P.O. Box 3966
>
> 1270 Fairfield Road, Suite 51
>
> Gettysburg, Pennsylvania 17325
>
> Telephone: (800) 344-7714 or (717) 338-1885
>
> Internet: www.cardtrak.com.
>
> (If you can't find information on its web site and you want the latest copy of its newsletter, send a $5 check payable to CardTrak.)

You can get information about your credit report from the three main credit reporting agencies (prices for a credit report vary based on where you live, so log on to one of the web sites or call to get the specific information for your state):

> Equifax
>
> Credit Information Services
>
> P.O. Box 105873
>
> Atlanta, Georgia 30348
>
> (800) 685-1111
>
> www.equifax.com

Experian

P.O. Box 2104

Allen, Texas 75013

(800) 682-7654

www.experian.com

Trans Union

Consumer Disclosure Center

P.O. Box 390

Springfield, PA 19064-0390

(800) 916-8800

www.transunion.com

The major credit card companies have proprietary sites:

American Express at www.americanexpress.com
Mastercard at www.mastercard.com
Visa at www.visa.com

For a bibliography of credit card info, check out:
www.creditcomm.com/reference/bccards.html

Shopping
For general information and links:

CompareNET at www.comparenet.com
   Carries product comparisons.

Consumer World at www.consumerworld.org
   This exhaustive site has links to a host of consumer sites on a range of topics.

For information on buying a car:

Edmund's Automobile Buyer's Guide at www.edmunds.com
National Buyers Federation at www.carquotes.com

The major long distance phone carriers:

AT&T at www.att.com
MCI at www.mci.com
Sprint at www.sprint.com

The Telecommunications Research and Action Center (a nonprofit organization) has useful information at www.trac.org

A few of the major computer manufacturers:

Apple at www.apple.com
Compaq at www.compaq.com
Dell at www.dell.com
Gateway at www.gateway.com

Consumer protection:

The Better Business Bureau at www.bbb.org
The Federal Trade Commission at www.ftc.gov
The National Fraud Information Center at www.fraud.org

Travel

Council on International Educational Exchange (Council Travel) at www.ciee.org

> This site has information on travel discounts, student identity cards, train travel, and general travel tips.

Hostelling International at www.hiayh.org

> Look here for information on hostels and membership.

Student Advantage at www.studentadvantage.com

> For details on membership and discounts.

Student Travel Agency at www.sta-travel.com

> You can get information on plane fares, student identity cards, and Eurail passes.

Some of the major travel guides (which have all kinds of interesting travel information):

Fodors at www.fodors.com
Let's Go at www.letsgo.com
Lonely Planet at www.lonelyplanet.com

The airlines:

America West at www.americawest.com
American at www.americanair.com
Carnival at www.carnivalair.com
Continental at www.flycontinental.com
Northwest at www.nwa.com
Southwest at www.iflyswa.com
TWA at www.twa.com
US Airways at www.usair.com

The car rental companies:

Alamo at www.goalamo.com
Avis at www.avis.com
Budget at www.budgetrentacar.com
Dollar at www.dollarcar.com
Enterprise at www.pickenterprise.com
Hertz at www.hertz.com
National at www.nationalcar.com

Online travel services (which have information on last-minute specials and let you make reservations):

Microsoft's travel service at www.expedia.com
Travelocity at www.travelocity.com

Tax information and forms:
Internal Revenue Service at www.irs.ustreas.gov
H&R Block at www.hrblock.com

Index

About the Author

Ellen Braitman is a journalist living in New York City. She is an assistant editor at *Consumer Reports* magazine and is frequently called upon by the media to speak about personal finance, including appearances on CNN and NBC's *Today*. Ellen graduated from Cornell University, where she was editor in chief of *The Cornell Daily Sun*. This book reflects her independent work done outside of *Consumer Reports*.